# The

# Devious Delinquents

## of

## Don and Marcia

## Upenleave

by

C J Upenleave

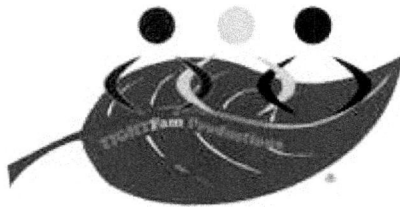

TIGHTFam Productions

# Devious Delinquents

Includes statistical and historic informational references:

The 25th Aviation Battalion website

dmh.mo.gov/fulton/history.htm


ISBN-13: 978-0988449800

ISBN-10: 0988449803

Edited by Marsha I. Stiles J.D.

Cover illustrations by : Phengsy Rattavong and C J Upenleave

Logo artwork by : Kam Reilly

The Best story is the One where I'm growing Old with my family!

This book was written with fond and loving memories of our father; Donald L.
Our grandparents; Fred and Adeline, Wilson and Rachael.
And a friend of the famly; Brooks H.


Special thanks to Mom, for tireless research and moral support.
Mary Palermo, Lisa Stevens and Vivian Forsythe
for their brutal, honest assessments of my first drafts.

# Table of Contents

Clockwise from left front : Philip, Steven, Donna, Christopher, Don, Fred, Teresa, Cynthia, Denise. Marcia is snapping the photo

# Foreword

My inspiration for this manuscript was a family history book written by Dorothy Tighe. Instead of chronologically plodding through the actions of her ancestors, leading up to the proceedings of her immediate family, chapter by chapter, she simply recalled humorous or adventurous tales. She too, had a surplus of family members whose gaffes inspired several short stories. With a little encouragement from my mother, I got motivated to start my own book with the purpose of preserving posterity. I used Dorothy's interior blueprint (short stories using family members as protagonists), yet my book differs from hers in the perspective that the stories are told. I thought it would be unique and engaging if the stories were written in a mixture of first and third person throughout, as if the entire Upenleave clan took turns penning the manuscript. Hopefully, a measure of intrigue will set in as you try to determine which one of us wrote the damn thing!

Our last name is fictitious, but as you progress through the book I think you'll agree that - it sure as hell fits!

As I said earlier, I started the book as a means of preserving posterity, but along the way I discovered that the stories being excavated would entertain and enlighten family and strangers alike.
Hopefully, after reading the book, you will have the enthusiasm and desire to pay it forward and the rest of us will revel in your family's personal history.

My wish is for you to turn the last page of this book and say to yourself, "I need to capture my family's priceless moments for posterity sake and share them with the world!" In your hands is the proof that such an endeavor is feasible. My family's priceless moments may not circulate to anyone outside my extended family. The same may be true of your family history book, but I am here to tell you . . . the journey embarked upon through each and every story and the relationships that blossom might turn out to be your most exhilarating and greatest accomplishment.

# Introduction

Time is never an ally when it comes to documenting deeds and adventures. It seems the longer you wait, the greater the chance of misconstruing events, grievous embellishment of stories or flat-out forgetting the details. In the recesses of the mind of each individual there lies a profusion of verbal treasures. When you have a family as large and loony as the one exposed in the following pages it is the Spanish Armada of verbal treasures. Sometimes it takes months to pry a juicy, shameful story from the lips of a singular creature even though you know damn well they are thinking about it right in front of you.

Relentless hounding and vicarious threats played a key role in the realization of this manuscript. Rest assured, I never followed through with the pet kidnappings or the vows of public humiliation that I threatened in the interest of getting stories from the protagonists of this manuscript. The hounding and threatening probably prolonged the project, but they most certainly did not detract from the enjoyment, stimulation and entertainment that I got out of it.

## Family Defined

Family is one of the few precious commodities remaining on our industrious planet that any person can have and hold no matter what your lineage has dealt you and regardless of your financial status. Despite your health and/or state of mind, on any given night you can be smack dab in the middle of a caring, supportive family. Conceivably I'm being a smidge overzealous with the whole family – commodity thing but I'm steadfast in the belief that a person who has a 'family' with which to share food, feelings and fun, goes through life with an enormous advantage over a person who chooses self-dependence. Your 'family' gives you an edge, makes you more attractive to others and, at the very least, facilitates somebody else to blame for your problems.

As for the unfortunate souls in this world who have few blood relatives or none at all, a 'family' can be anybody you choose to spend time with: a church group, a neighbor, a book club. All you have to do is make the effort to show up and engage them with an open mind and a kind heart.

If you are spending more than twenty-four waking hours per week alone, I urge you to take the initiative in seeking out people whom you might enjoy spending time with.

Use some common sense here. If you're a 45 year old single male don't barge into an in vitro fertilization seminar expecting a warm welcome and hugs all around.

## In a Nutshell

A family works together, plays together, makes fun of each other. scolds one another, heralds victories, encourages resolve in failures, shares everything. They will do absolutely anything for you. As I was writing this very page my 13 year-old daughter said, "You know something, the world needs a family."

What will it take to reverse the greed, intolerance and bloodshed  that has riddled our planet since the creation of man. Maybe . . . a chain of family history books will be the catapult to the era of reconciliation and harmony on Earth. Hey, it was only a few centuries ago when electricity was an impossible dream!

# The Beginning

## Who's My Date?

Marcia was the oldest of Wilson and Rachael's three children. They lived in a small but sufficient home in an average neighborhood in Monona, Wisconsin. Quiet and unassuming, mom was seventeen when her friend Shirley talked her into going on a blind date.

Two high school girls met a couple of Air Force boys at Renenbaum's Drug Store for some food and frolic.

Don Upenleave must have been on his best behavior because soon after, he and Marcia had a couple more casual get-togethers at Marcia's parents' house.

Wilson and Rachael would have preferred mom date someone who wasn't six years her senior, and Marcia's grandma didn't like him one bit, but that didn't deter Don from trying to call on her every chance he . . . *not so fast, Romeo, the military owns your hide*. He packed his bags and shipped out for a three month training class in California.

Sunny Cali put a damper on Don's courting plan but, he tried to make the most of his involuntary hiatus by saving up a tidy sum of cash and sending mom a dozen roses to make sure she didn't forget about him. Three months of training to be a military cop seemed to drag on forever. Upon his return, they planned a date at a popular Chinese restaurant.

At last, the day arrived. Don checked back into the Air Force base near Monona and as soon as he was clear of his duties, put on his slickest suit, made a reservation for two at the hippest Chinese restaurant in town and called his sweetheart to firm up the date.

She was ready! He picked her up at her parents' house and they cruised into town. When they got to the restaurant, it was obviously a popular place. Good thing they had a reservation. Don requested a table with a little privacy, and as soon as they were seated dad inquired, "Did you like the roses?"

"Oh! They were from you?" was mom's instinctive reply.

*So much for the Sweet and Sour Chicken!*

The onset of the date was definitely sweet, but Don's emotions got the best of him so he ushered her home in silence and the evening ended sourly with Don wishing Marcia to "have a swell life!"

Of course they were married three months later.

But first, mom graduated high school and weathered the storm of her parents' disapproval since accepting dad's marriage proposal. Marcia's life was on the verge of an ABOUT FACE! The simple life was behind her now.

They hopped on a train to Kansas City where Marcia met Don's parents, Fred and Adeline. Don was the oldest of six. The two youngest children lived with Don's parents in a four room apartment.

Needless to say, the eager couple did not overstay their welcome and were married in Grandview, Missouri a few days later. The honeymoon consisted of Dad packing his uniforms for his first permanent duty station, Sculthorpe Air Base, UK where he would finish his training and fulfill his duties as a military policeman.

Mom stayed in Monona with her parents for a month or so while dad got settled in and secured a home for his bride. He wrote and expressed his excitement about the place he found just off base and how anxious he was to have her there. Mom shared his enthusiasm and couldn't wait to start a new adventure with him.

When the day arrived, she said a tearful goodbye to her loving family and took a flight to the East coast.
From there she boarded a military troop transport ship and took a week long voyage across the Atlantic Ocean.

If you ever had the pleasure of sailing aboard a troop transport ship as early as 1955, you would know that it was sort of like a cruise liner . . . minus the cruise, and with plenty of lines to stand in: single file to get your meals, along the bulkhead in the hallway to get into the store, and waiting patiently for a nearby shower to become available.

Midway through the voyage the ship was ravaged by gale-force winds. For three days mom, and the women who shared her small cabin, subsisted on sips of water. Everything else just came back up.

**England - 1955**

LAND HO! Not a moment too soon. Mother fled the troop transporter into the awaiting arms of her adoring husband. After a long, passionate kiss he whisked her away to a place he called home.
Mom paused to admire the two story house before entering the threshold. She was all smiles as she stepped inside and viewed the kitchen on the right, the living room on the left and the staircase in front of her.
"This is pretty nice, honey. It's a little crude, but we'll manage to dress it up a bit. You did a great job!" she emphasized as she requested another hug.
        "Hey! Hey! Do I hear another voice down there?" Came a deep voice from upstairs.
Mom jumped out of dad's arms and turned to see another couple bounding down the stairs with gleeful smirks like Marcia was Elizabeth Taylor.

"You must be Marcia." The man spouted, thrusting his hand within inches of her bosom. Hesitantly, she shook his hand. There was no hiding her look of bewilderment.

"This is Ted and Betty, hon." Dad interjected. "They live upstairs."

Mom was too busy praying that this was some sort of newlywed prank or pay-back for the roses incident to hear a single word the annoying couple were blathering at her. Her eyes quickly scanned the place again and her instincts were correct. There wasn't one freaking door to allow them a sliver of privacy. That's when she fainted.

"Oh my God!" Betty shrieked . "The trip was too much for her, poor thing. Don't just stand there like a couple of boobs . . . someone go get a cool, damp wash cloth!"

"I don't think I have a wash cloth," dad sputtered. "Will a sponge do?"

"Is it clean?" Betty snarled.

"Sure. I've just used it on the sink and the tub."

"I'll go get a wash cloth! What the hell are you men good for?"

Ted looked at dad. Dad looked at Ted.

"Let's carry her to the bathroom." Dad suggested.

They agreed and got her in on the bathroom floor in a matter of seconds. That's what men are good for!

They also excel at making quick, crude decisions. like when dad began splashing mom's face with small amounts of cold water from the bath tub.

Sure she would have to change her blouse when this ordeal was over, but her eyes fluttered open and she licked her wet lips as Betty scurried in with the wash cloth. Dad helped her sit up and there was complete silence as she got her bearings. Her eyes focused on the doorway, then she spoke. "Thank God . . . there's a door for the bathroom."

The refrigerator . . . did not exist. They would have to make do with an ice box. A washing machine wasn't part of the deal. There was no central heat, but there was a fireplace in practically every room, a coke-fired stove hooked up to the water heater and a door on the bathroom. It was Don and Marcia Upenleave's first home. They were happy and grateful to be together with a roof over their heads.

A year later, on December 13th 1956, their first child was born. Her hair was so long and dark the proud parents clairvoyantly named her after a 1970s brother and sister pop duo.
Donna Marie made Don a proud papa. On duty days, he took Donna to the barracks to meet the fellas and he snapped pictures of her every day.

Donna was an easy infant. Up at 6:00 every morning and ready for a nap at noon. Mom liked to fire up a cigarette a few dozen times a day, but not indoors, so she bundled Donna and set her outside in a buggy to enjoy the fresh air and the bird droppings. This routine might have had something to do with Donna's tendencies as an adult to constantly check the sky above her and become nauseous at the sight of anything white and creamy.

On December 22nd 1957, came their second child. The boy was named after both grandfathers, Fred Martin (Martin was Wilson's middle name).

Everyone has had some adversity in their life. Freddy was born into it! He had to be resuscitated immediately. It was anyone's guess how long he had gone without breathing. It took a few repetitions of baby CPR, but Freddy finally came to life with authority! His lungs were operating at peak levels within seconds. Mom and dad counted their blessings and thanked the Lord for a baby boy with the possibility of a career in opera.

Freddy's appetite fluctuated in his early years. Mom spent weeks trying to experiment with the mixture of his formula and get to the root cause of his inconsistent eating habits. After three months of frustration, the truth was revealed.
The pediatrician's staff had given mom a formula mixture that was way too strong for a baby. When they realized their mistake and tried to feed Freddy the correct mixture, it was too late.
He could not be satisfied with the weak-ass baby formula that he was supposed be taking. His response was oohh hell no! Get me back on the good stuff, PRONTO, followed by constant whining and crying.

## Back to the States

Father soon realized that advancing his rank (which equates to earning higher pay) as an Air Force military policeman would be difficult so he made the switch to working on transponders. Transponders identify aircraft as being friend or foe on a pilots radar screen and provide distance and attitude information. This resulted in his transfer to another training facility, Kessler AFB, Mississippi.

Meanwhile, mother was pregnant again. Around the beginning of her third trimester, my parents knew the right thing to do was to get mom stateside as soon as possible. Dad took on the burden of the move, which was provided by the military.

Mom would stay with her parents in Wisconsin until Dad was able to meet her and migrate to Mississippi with his family.

Their third child was born in mom's home town, Monona, Wisconsin. Cynthia Louise was born on December 23rd 1958.
Mother was grateful to have her family to support her and help take care of Donna and Freddy.

The birth was much smoother than Freddy's and Marcia hoped that baby Cynthia would be more content as well. Of course, mother and children were welcomed in Wilson and Rachael's home, but mom was worried that a fussy baby would surely heighten the tension in an overcrowded house.

Baby Cindy was a little princess . . . and her kingdom was known as colic! The princess of colic was especially fond of disturbing the tranquility of a good night sleep. Everyone knows that colic usually lasts two or three months. They loved their daughter and grandkids, but Wilson and Rachael were secretly hoping that their daughter would be joining her husband in Mississippi yesterday, if not sooner!

Unfortunately for our grandparent's, this was only PART ONE of The Homeless Upenleave's.
It wasn't anyone's fault that we were homeless (as far as we knew). The housing on Kessler Air Force base was limited because it was a training facility.

Dad was busy learning a new trade, living in the barracks and waiting for a house to become available for us.

Well, Princess Cindy took so much pride in her kingdom that she carried out her duties well past the day that dad was able to bring us south. There was a mixture of emotions in the tears of grandpa and grandma this time.

There were sad to see us go, hopeful that a reunion was in the near future; yet ecstatic to finally be rescued!

# Southern Hospital´

## Gulfport, Mississippi – 1959

The drive to Gulfport, Mississippi would have been uneventful, if not for two adverse events. First, the car's generator failed outside of Chicago. Lucky for us, mom's Uncle, Forrest lived in the area and let us stay the night. Forrest had no idea that mom and dad didn't have the money to pay for the repair and that's the way it stayed. Forrest dropped us off at the mechanic's shop the next day and headed into work.

The owner of the repair shop was headstrong and tight fisted. He was dead-set on being paid in-full before surrendering the keys.
  "Sorry folks. No exceptions. You can use the pay phone outside to scare up some cash, there's some doughnuts on my desk over there and the crapper is outside on the North wall."

Mom and dad were stuck. They had already borrowed $40.00 from Marcia's parents for the trip.

The only solution they came up with was to call dad's new unit at Kessler and try to get someone or some institution to float them a loan until payday. Dad camped next to the payphone in the cold drizzle while Mom, little Cynthia, Freddy and Donna took up the entire waiting room.

16

Freddy had no opinion about this predicament.
Donna was becoming more restless by the minute.
Princess Cynthia made it abundantly clear that
she was not fond of dirt, grease, hammering
noises, stale doughnuts or a filthy crapper. She
gave the owner a sample of the power of her
kingdom and within an hour the garage owner was
acting like Barney Fife trying to disarm a time
bomb.
He summoned dad into his office, wrote down his
military info, accepted half of the amount and
hurried us on our way. Mom actually mailed the
remainder of the debt to the garage owner within a
couple of months.

The second adverse event happened in Gulfport,
Mississippi. Our parents unloaded some
belongings at their house then went straight to the
grocery store with a few dollars to spend. Mother
was inside the supermarket while father was being
entertained by us kids in the car.

After a few minutes had passed a disturbing noise
came from Freddy that sounded like he was
struggling to breathe. When dad leaned into the
back seat to check on him he got a flashback of
Freddy's birth! No telling how long Freddy had
stopped breathing normally, but there was no time
to waste! He snatched him from the safety seat
and sprinted across the parking lot with the limp
baby boy in his arms.

The supermarket employees were quick to notice
the man cradling a limp infant yelling "Help, call
for an ambulance!"

Mom recognized the distressed man's voice dropped her groceries and found them in seconds. When she saw the color of her baby boy she knew exactly what she had to do. An employee hastened her to the nearest water fountain where she began splashing his face with cold water. Marcia's little boy was drenched and still not responding so she resorted to a typical loving mother's resuscitation technique - slapping the snot out of him. Shoppers thought there was a couple of stock boys scrapping near the water cooler and flocked to the action.

The emergency crew arrived just when Freddy came to life with a welcome wail. Sighs of relief and emotional tears followed as the crew ushered momma and baby into the awaiting ambulance. Freddy went to the hospital, but was released soon after.

The doctors involved had no specific diagnosis and Freddy appeared to have no immediate repercussions.

Welcome to Gulfport! It was 1959 and Mississippi had passed the Civil Rights Act, the first step to securing the right to vote for blacks in the South. Congratulations, Don and Marcia! You've just won an all expenses paid extended-stay trip to the hotbed of racial tension in the South!

Fortunately their stay was transitory because Kessler Air Force Base was just a training facility. Despite the pleasant weather, mother was happy to move on.

Dad's next duty station was Biggs Air Force Base in El Paso, Texas. We were looking forward to hunkering down in one spot for a while. For most people "a while" equates to about a decade, but for us, three years was plenty. Certainly enough time for a young Catholic couple to add three (*yes, three*) more young-uns to the litter. Denise was the first born in El Paso, January 1960. Next came Steven, February 1961 and finally Philip, February 1962.

1960
Dad's holding farmgirl Denise
Donna is in the middle
Mom's holding the hat thief, Cindy
Fred is a towhead?

# Are These All Yours?

Let's recap, shall we? Don and Marcia Upenleave married in 1955 and by March of 1962 had six healthy children, one each year. The math is simple and the data does not lie. During that eighty six month span, mom was pregnant for 54 months doing arguably the hardest job in the world (raising several kids). We're not talking about pumping them out, adding another name to the welfare rolls and living a life based on her recreational needs. Marcia's life WAS her children. She was pregnant 62.8 % of the time.

JFK became president in 1961. Being devout Catholics, my parents were very optimistic about the leadership and future of our country.

Where were we now? Oh yes, El Paso,1962. Being in the Air Force did not guarantee a person to being stationed comfortably in the states. There was a war raging in Viet Nam. The 25th Aviation Battalion website states that our government tripled the number of military troops in Vietnam in 1961 and tripled them again in 1962. Dad's number was called and he reported for duty in March of '62.

Denise was two, Steve was one and Phil had been eating, sleeping and pooping for only a few weeks, but, mother professed that so far, Denise had been the easiest baby of the bunch. One day a neighbor lady was visiting during nap time.

Marcia was ironing clothes and the two women had been chatting and gossiping for at least thirty minutes when the lady was startled by something at her feet. It was baby Denise, who had been in the room and gone unnoticed by the neighbor lady the entire time.

Dad was just an E4 in the Air Force so his send home pay reeeeeeeally had to be stretched, pulled and groped to last until the end of the month. Every nickel counted. Mom wrote to her parents in Wisconsin weekly. There were times when she had to ask for a small handout to make it through the month, even when her father was unemployed.

Christmas was practically the only time of the year when someone in our family got something new. Of course there were exceptions: necessary clothes and shoes for us kids, but only for the ones who couldn't fit into hand-me-downs.

This was the era when five year old Donna, the oldest child, was still too young to watch after the rest of us sooooo . . . can you imagine being Marcia in the grocery store? Undoubtedly a chore that she tried to accomplish just once a month.

One day the neighbors across the street from our house in El Paso bought an appliance and left the box in their front yard. Mom was whistling cheerfully as she cleaned the nearly empty, quiet house and we kids played outside.
The doorbell chimed and a strange elderly woman was standing on our porch. "Can I help you?" Mom inquired.

"I hope so," was the old woman's reply. "I can't get through this street to get to my bingo game."

Mother stepped outside and immediately spotted the box in the middle of the street. She also noticed that her children were nowhere in sight.

"Oh my goodness! Did you happen to see some small children playing nearby?"

The old woman motioned for mom to follow. She ambled out to the middle of the street where they both peered into a box full of giggling kids. Mom scolded Donna (5) and Fred (4) as she lifted Cindy (3) out. Donna pushed the box over from the inside while mom was placing Cindy in the yard. Donna and Freddy slithered out and joined their sister in the yard as mother dragged the box back to the neighbor's house.

"Are these all yours?" The old woman asked.

"Yes, with three more sleeping inside."

"Well, thank you and . . . good luck!" With that the elderly lady was off to her bingo game.

**Texas Two Hop**

During the next five to six years our family continued the nomadic tendencies. You might even say the bar was raised a couple of notches.

First we went back to Wisconsin shortly after dad left for Viet Nam and stayed with mom's parents until dad returned in October of 1963.
James Connelly Air Base was our next duty station. It was seven miles from Waco Texas. We got settled in just in time to be devastated by the assassination of our beloved President in Dallas. I have a visual memory of my mom weeping for days while doing her housework.

We were in Waco for three years during which, after a three year respite, dad got mom pregnant again. Teresa Jean was born on November 14th 1965. As was the custom, Teresa was not allowed the opportunity to get familiar with her birth place.

Five year old Denise married her short-time sweetheart, Dana (the cute neighbor boy), in the garage. The ceremony was fleeting yet magnificent! Denise's blanket (*I mean dress*), captured the eye with vivid colors and slightly tattered edges.

All she could manage to do was stand and wobble in mom's high heels. Denise's dolls were propped up on benches and boxes being particularly well-behaved.

Nine year old Donna presided over the blossoming couple with the "do you takes" and the "you may now kiss my sister . . . with pursed lips", while the rest of us (and some friends) witnessed the implausible affair through the garage window and teased Denise forever afterwards.

## Growing up

By this time, Donna and Fred were going to school. Donna struggled a bit with reading and math, but tried very hard. She got an allowance of 15 cents a week for making her bed in the morning, drying the dishes at night and cleaning her room on Saturday. She usually had to be reminded and/or hounded to accomplish the latter. Her struggles with reading continued through the third grade, but she had become quite the take-charge little helper that mother needed.

Fred surpassed Donna in reading but was slower than most of his classmates in math and science. He had constantly harked to mom that he wasn't going to school next year! He slept on the top bunk in the boys' room and made sure the room was neat and organized. Fred was the trash man too. He enjoyed playing outside, but took no interest in the backyard sports games that most of the neighborhood boys couldn't wait to do after school.

Cindy had turned out to be the most independent so far. By independent I mean stubborn. She liked to do things *her* way. Typically, for a middle child, she was boisterous yet easily influenced by anyone who gave her recognition. Frequent asthma attacks and ear infections hampered her growth.

Denise was pretty healthy, kind of quiet but didn't take any crap from her elder siblings. She liked to dress up and play with dolls, but also loved to get muddy.

Steve was rough and ready. He had already broken his collar bone twice by the age of five. He had a big heart though. In kindergarten Steve helped a little girl at school who was holding up the line on the tall slide because she was too scared to go down. Regrettably, the fall broke her arm.

Philip was very small at four years. His appetite had been a pittance of a normal boy's, most likely due to the bouts of bronchitis he was constantly battling. Phillip was just beginning to talk and seemed to like tagging along with Steve, until things got rough.

We were true brothers and sisters. We were growing together, forming bonds, becoming enemies for a few hours and going almost everywhere together.

left to right, back row: Cindy, Denise, Fred, Donna. Front row: Steve, Phil

## The Aquarium

Dad's pride and joy in Waco, Texas was his five
foot, 40 gallon, fresh-water fish tank. It was
captivating and calming. Just what the doctor
ordered for this sometimes frenzied bunch.
Dad chose an exceptionally colorful array of fish
and everyone at some point was lured in close to
gaze at the fluid, agile movements orchestrated
within inches of their nose.
Mom was an admirer at first, but after the third
tank cleaning her attitude shifted more toward
the; *I hate this stinking aquarium* perspective.

It was a mid-summer day. Mom and dad were busy
while a few of us kids (and some friends) were
running through the house, shouting, laughing
and playing. It was mayhem light because dad and
mom were pre-occupied. Mom would have put the
kibosh on the parade immediately. Dad would
have been a little more forgiving, but eventually,
would have nipped it as well. It was a peculiar day,
then there was a crash. It was the sound of glass
breaking and water gushing. Everyone in ear-shot
scampered into the living room. Well, we can only
assume that everyone who heard the smash and
gush was present at the scene, for the perpetrator
was never pinpointed. Maybe the delinquent just
kept moving when it crashed then weaseled into
the crowd or walked away casually. Someone
running from the scene would surely have been
fingered. Whatever the case, it went down as
another unsolved mystery.

Parting was such sweet sorrow. Don said a petulant goodbye to his colorful fish and the only aquarium our family would ever purchase.

We would eventually have fish in our home again, but our house would function as the aquarium. That is another circumstance in a different state altogether.

Soon afterwards, mom and dad decided that they liked it better in El Paso. Poor, little Denise. She was only five years old and already suffered from a broken heart, because we relocated to El Paso in 1966. But only for a brief stay.

# Spin the Bottle

## El Paso, Texas – 1966

At some point in El Paso mom took a part-time job and hired a Latino maid to help with the housework. This situation created a helpful environment for nine year old Donna and her friends to 'get to know' some of the neighborhood boys.

Delight was Donna's best friend. Both were nine. Delight and her sisters, Star and Melody, lived a couple of blocks away. Star (7) was Cindy's age and Melody (5) Steve's age.

On occasions when the maid was the only adult in the house, Donna and Delight transformed the garage into a boy kissing festival!
When I say garage, even though it's irrelevant, I should clarify that the architectural genius who designed the house put siding with a large sliding glass door on the front of the garage. So it wasn't a car garage, it was more like . . . a spin the bottle (SpB) room with a smooth concrete floor.

Normally, Donna and Delight would stand on a nearby street corner until one of the neighborhood boys came into view. Then they would whistle or wave to attract his attention. The first boy that they reeled in would usually be willing to go recruit some of his friends and hustle back!

Apparently it was easy for Donna and Delight to lure three or four of the local boys aspiring to be Justin Bieber into the SpB room.

It wasn't always the same boys. In fact, Donna and Delight were partial to a healthy variety.

The girls and the game, however, remained the same. Donna would bribe Cindy and Denise with goods or services, whatever it took, while Delight would recruit Star into joining them for the sake of getting as many boys as possible into the affair. Cindy would resist despite the possibility of kissing a cute, older boy. She was only eight afterall.
Denise was care-free.

We all know how to play spin the bottle. In this case, the person the bottle pointed to had to go into the storage room at the back of the SpB room.

The bottle was spun again until it pointed to someone of the opposite gender, who would then join the first person in the storage room. The couple in the storage room could leave the light on, or turn it off, depending on the level of nervousness. They were also free to do anything that the girl would allow or act upon. The people sitting in a circle on the floor would determine the length of time for each intimate encounter.

*Did mom ever find out about the game?* Not until the girls were too old to be locked in their room. (*As if that would have deterred them*). Ha!

# Haunted House

## El Paso, Texas - 1967

There was an abandoned house in the neighborhood that all the neighbor kids swore was haunted. Of course there was no merit to the allegations, but when a few of the older kids claimed they saw a man in the upstairs window, things got a little more interesting.

The abandoned house was right next door to Delight, Star and Melody's house. Fred (9) and Star were walking in the middle of the street in front of Star's house when Howard, another nine year old neighborhood boy, jogged over to them.

"Hey, Freddie, guess what? Me and Jimmy found an unlocked window in the back of the empty house. I bet you're too scared to go in there, aren't you?" Howard grinned and winked at Star. Star was completely unimpressed, but held her tongue, allowing Fred to counter.

"My name is Fred," he corrected. "Why didn't you guys go in?"

"Oh, uhhhh . . . Jimmy had to go home."

"Ok. That was his excuse. What's yours?" Fred's honesty was brutal. One of his innate qualities was to remind people that they weren't fooling anybody and it didn't matter whose feelings were tromped on.

"I'm just saying, I bet you're too scared to go in there!" Howard dared.

"What, in broad daylight?"

Steve (6) had just been given permission to play outside and had been looking around the neighborhood for some friends. He just happened to find Fred at that very moment. Steve waved from a distance then jogged over to join him.

"What's goin' on guys?"

"I'm not a guy." Star reminded Steve.

"Wanna do something cool, Steve?" Fred prompted.

"Sure."

A smart boy would have asked what it was first, but Steve was not destined for intellectual prowess. He was a boy of action!

They all talked about the deed for a few more minutes then swept briskly to the back of the house, where, Howard the coward helped Fred and Steve climb through the window that Star held open.

Fred and Steve meandered cautiously through the two-story house room-by-room. There was no furniture downstairs, no belongings and no critters. Trash scattered here and there was the only thing that stood out, so they decided to embark on an upstairs assessment. When they arrived at the top of the stairs, Fred wanted to expedite the assessment, so he insisted that Steve go a separate direction. Of course, Steve would have preferred to trail Fred the entire way, but he didn't want Fred to know that he was scared shitless!

Fred eased into the first room on the left while Steve moved down the right side of the hall.

The first room Steve peeked into had a rocking chair in it . . . that was rocking all by itself. Steve darted down the hall and leaped down the stairs in a single bound. He almost cleared the stairs. His heels slid off the second step, he tumbled to the floor then WHAM! The wall stopped him.

Fred heard the racket and made a pretty fast exit himself, without the self-inflicting stair leap. When Fred got to the first floor, Steve was rattling off some drivel about a rocking chair as he tried to figure out how to unlock the front door.

When he finally got it open there was a small crowd of kids from ages five to fifteen standing in the front yard. The two brothers were greeted by a hearty round of applause. Steve transformed from a blithering chicken-shit to a brave hero faster than his stairwell leap! All were anxious to hear about the puddle of blood, the noose in the closet, or the strange unearthly gadget in the bathroom.

"Nothing in there but a little bit of trash and a lot of dust," exclaimed Fred.

"And a rocking, rocking chair!" Steve blurted.

He scanned the group for a sign that somebody would be curious about the rocking chair but it was if they didn't even hear him. The party was over. Everyone went their separate ways murmuring their acceptance of Fred's findings. No one else wanted to venture inside.

A week passed. It was a typical warm summer evening. Star was alone in her backyard when her parents were jolted by her blood-curdling screams. They raced outside and couldn't help noticing a car speeding away without headlights. They found Star wedged deep into a thorny bush, eyes wide with shock. Deftly, they eased her from its raw, torturous, grip. Bloody and panicky, Star still managed to explain how she got there.

"I was just playing around . . . when all of the sudden this man crawled out of the window of the abandoned house. I watched him run towards me but he hadn't seen me yet. I froze, hoping he wouldn't. He was carrying a bag or a case or something. I ducked down but before I knew it he jumped over the wall and grabbed me. I was too scared to scream."
Star swallowed hard and took a deep breath.
"He put my face really close to his and told me to keep my mouth shut or he would come back and kill us." She sobbed uncontrollably as her parents soothed and hugged her. "Mom, I'll never forget his awful breath!"

The incident was the buzz of the neighborhood for quite a while and Star became somewhat of a celebrity but nobody ever solved the mystery. Who? What? or Why?

Our Texas paradise ended a few months later. Dad got transferred to Eglin Air Force Base near Ft. Walton Beach, Florida.

# First Knives

## Fort Walton Beach, Florida - 1967

The 1967 Christmas in Florida was a memorable one for Fred (10) and Steve (6) because dad and mom gave them their first pocket knives. The girls looked on curiously, wondering if this was a good idea as the boys fumbled with their dangerous prizes. A sense of responsibility had been bestowed on them with this gift. Don's instructions were clear, "these are whittling and wood carving knives, boys. They are not to be used like toys or swords in some make-believe joust."

When the morning celebrations were complete, the two boys eagerly escaped to the nearby woods to find a stick or a branch with which to christen their knives. It was close to thirty minutes of sharpening branches into weapons before Steve became totally bored with that routine. Shows like Wild, Wild, West and Daniel Boone were proof to Steve that a knife, if thrown properly, would stick into an object precisely where you aimed it. The tree in front of him would suffice as his first target. Despite Fred's warnings, Steve held the blade just above his ear, straightened his arm and flicked his wrist. The knife twirled, end-to-end . . . right past the tree and into the sand behind it. Steve shrugged and Fred laughed as they went to the spot where the knife landed. There was no sign of it so Steve started digging in the soft, sandy dirt. He dug and searched, then persuaded Fred to help him search and dig, but to no avail.

Steve was panicked and Fred was being righteous with "I told you not to," as they made their way home.

Steve feared the worst of father's retribution, but dad was surprisingly calm and willing to help Steve search for his new Christmas gift. Dad requested that Fred join them, so Fred reluctantly tagged along.

That was good thinking on dad's part because after a lengthy search of the area where the boys swore the knife landed, dad was scratching his head. His only other alternative was to try and duplicate the incident, so with Fred's knife, Steve stood exactly where he thought he was, held Fred's knife just as he had held his own, and hurled it end-over-end past the tree and into the area where they had been fruitlessly digging. Dad and Fred watched closely and hurried to the spot where the knife made impact with the earth.

Once again there was no sign of it. After some digging, dad unearthed a long, slender rock. He dug some more and persuaded the boys to dig in too (no pun intended). Together they managed to dig up a six foot square area where the shallowest point was a foot deep, but with raw fingers and empty pockets, they gave up the search and accepted defeat at the hands of the mysterious sandy forest, which, as it turned out, held more surprises.

So the boys' never really got to use their prized
Christmas gifts and dad's decision to duplicate
Steve's bad judgment became one of mom's favorite
stories to tell among friends and relatives when
she felt that her hubbie needed a little dose of
humility.


**Dancing with Himself**

Our house at Eglin Air Force Base (Fort Walton
Beach), Florida was a duplex. It just so happened
that there were a couple of boys around Donna (11)
and Cindy's (9) age living next door.

It was a Saturday and Donna had fulfilled all of
her school and home chores. She was headed to
Teen Town! Eglin Air Force Base had a
recreational building where teens could shoot pool,
play pinball and dance to D. J. music. This was
unequivocally Donna's favorite spot on earth!
Everybody who was anybody showed up for the
dancing at 11:00 AM on Saturday. Her outfit for
the event was a no-brainer, a slam-dunk! What
else would she wear to her favorite spot on earth
but her most beloved blue dress with white lace
sleeves that flared out like bell bottom jeans at the
wrist. Under her dress she wore white fish-net
stockings and, of course, her slickest dance shoes.
When it came to style, Donna was a guru. She
moved some clothes in her closet to find her dress
and found something she wasn't expecting . . . a
nail hole in the closet wall that allowed a single
beam of light to invade the darkness.

Donna was never one to let her curiosity linger. On the other side of the wall was the neighbor boy's room.

The tiny circumference of the hole greatly restricted the scenery. All she could make out was a boy walking past her peep hole. She was pretty sure the lead of her pencil would fit into that hole. If she pushed real hard and twisted it she could make the hole bigger. Voila! Now she could see a little more of what was going on in there. Her eye was scanning for clues like she was looking through a telescope and just discovered an open window to the Beatles dressing room. Funny, it just occurred to her that she had been living there for almost six months and he had not spoken a word to her. She knew damn well he wasn't mute. He wasn't in her fifth grade class, but she saw him at school all the time, jabbering with friends in the hallways.

Suddenly, Donna felt pressure on her back. She recoiled against the wall like a safe robber caught red-handed.

"Geez, Donna, why are you so jumpy?" Cindy pried.

"You scared the heck out of me, twerp!"

"Hey, I never noticed that hole before. What were you looking at?" Cindy had to bend down just slightly to get her eye on it. She scanned for a second then got a hot target lock and whispered anxiously "Oh my God! There's a boy undressing in there."

Donna's eyebrows elevated.

She nodded gently then shoved Cindy aside and occupied the peep hole in time to see him throw his shirt on the floor and get a clean one. "Hmmm, Donna jeered, are you ready to go to Teen Town?"

"Yep." Cindy smiled.

"Is Fred coming with us?" Donna wondered.

"I think so. He's watching TV . . . waiting for us."

So the three elders struck out for Teen Town where the action was infinite and the mischief was deep.

As for the peep hole, Donna and Cindy spied on the boy next door for almost two weeks before he realized he was the entertainment. One day he heard them talking and put his eye to the hole. He caught a glimpse of the girls, fleeing like he was the cootie king.

It was a strange relationship that evolved through the peep hole. When he was aware of them, he would play music and dance, try acrobatic tricks, which would lead to him spilling or knocking something over. He never spoke to the girls nor they to him. Even when they saw each other outside, a wave would usually suffice. Neither of the girls recall his name, so he will forever be remembered as the peep hole boy.

## Pain in the Back

The woods close to our home in Florida provided a natural getaway for we kids to explore and play games.

Fred, Cindy, Denise, and Phil were making their way home from one such activity when Fred complained of pain in his back. As a rule, when a kid complains about something hurting, the other kids either ignore him or call him a sissy. Since it was Fred's first whine, they just ignored him.

They were out of the woods and getting close to home when Fred scratched his back, then abruptly yelped and jerked his hand away.
"What's going on?" Denise asked.
"Something's killing my back." Fred grimaced.
"Don't be such a wuss!" Cindy scolded.
"You should take your shirt off," Phil advised.
But they kept on trucking. Soon the house was in view and they could see mother sweeping the front porch. She spotted them and waited.

The moment they were in earshot Fred bellowed, "Mom! Something's hurting my back!"
"Did you fall down?"
"Nope!"
"Turn around and put your arms up."

Fred complied. Mom pulled his shirt off, shook it out and down on the porch plopped a scorpion that appeared to be ready for a fight to the death, pinchers gnashing and stinger curled in tight - ready to strike!

WHAM! The bad ass scorpion caught the business end of mom's broom. WHAM! WHAM! WHAM! WHAM! WHAM! Quick battle. Game over.

Everyone peered down at the intact but flattened scorpion. It was light brown, and about two inches long. Everyone peered up at Fred writhing there with his mouth agape. Once again, Fred appeared to be doomed. From what we had seen on T.V., scorpions were deathly poisonous and Fred had SIX welts at various spots on his back.

Mother hastened to the phone. While she was talking to the doctor, Denise, Cindy and Phil hovered around Fred, firing important questions at him.
>"Are you gonna puke?"
>"Should we put it in a jar for you?"
>"Can I have your etch a sketch . . . when you're,  you know?"

Mom took Fred to the doctor who determined that there was no eminent danger.
Fred's appetite suffered slightly as did his sleep for the next few nights because his loving brothers and sisters took turns waking him up in the middle of the night to make sure he was still alive.

## Ahhhh the Beach

The Florida Beaches remain some of the most memorable getaway spots for our family. The most memorable incident occurred mid-day on a gorgeous weekend.

A park on Eglin Air Force Base backed right up to the gulf where a roped off beach area was located.

Normally there would be only a handful of military families, but on this magnificent day, the beach area was teeming with individuals whose translucent skin was the only evidence needed to conclude - that it was their first time this year.

Mother and father were relaxing on a blanket in the sand while the six of us splashed and swam along with approximately 40 other folks. Well, most people wouldn't call watching six children, from 5 to 10 years old, swim in the ocean, relaxing. They're right. Dad and mom were propped up on a blanket in the sand chatting while maintaining vigilant eyes on the swim area.

Donna was the only decent swimmer. Fred professed to be capable, but the gamut of his strokes consisted of the you're a peein' dogpaddle. That was pretty much it. The other four just stayed where they could touch the bottom.

Donna wanted to swim out to the deep area with the help of a colorful beach ball.
All she had to do was kick those legs and she had instant propulsion.

The snag in this superb family outing surfaced when the beach ball squirted away from Donna, who was moving toward the deep end. For some reason this became the perfect opportunity for Fred to display some heroics. He bounced confidently off the sandy bottom and retrieved the toy floaty.

He was making his way back toward the beach when, all at once, Fred was no longer bouncing. In fact, he was gone. He had hit a drop-off that was in the middle of the swimming area and went down like Charlie Brown's Halloween sack. When he emerged his dogpaddle was frantic. He was struggling to keep his head above water and losing the battle, so he reached out and volunteered Donna to save his ass by pulling himself up on top of her.

Fred was gasping for air, holding on to Donna's neck and shoulders for dear life while Donna was holding her breath underwater trying to fight him off.

My parents saw the turbulence in the water and were quick to recognize none other than Fred Upenleave smack in the middle of it.

They sprinted across the sand then high-stepped the shallow water until it was deep enough for them to dive. Once dad was prone on the water he showed everyone how to do the 'save my kids' stroke.

It was strange how nobody in the water at the time tried to help the distressed pair.

They sure as hell got out of dad's way as he created a wake to get there.

Dad finally made it within reach of them, but Donna was not in sight, so he just grabbed Fred and flung him back toward the beach. As soon as Fred was displaced, Donna's arm breached the surface. Dad quickly got her head above water.

When Fred landed with a splash mom wrapped her arm around him and towed him to shore. Dad did the same with Donna, but she was dead weight and darn near lifeless. It seemed as if it took 100 times longer for dad to get back to shore with Donna. His military training included CPR and it only took a single cycle of pumps and breaths for Donna to heave out the water she had swallowed and start breathing on her own. It was another close call, but our family was still intact.

Dad lost his watch during the rescue and Fred suffered minor bruises . . . when Donna got her strength back! Other than that, it was just a normal family outing at the beach!

Alas, the family's beach getaways were terminated indefinitely when dad received orders to report to Okinawa in December of 1968.

# Three Months at Grandpa's House

## Monona, Wisconsin - 1968

When dad went to Okinawa, mom once again migrated to where she felt most comfortable - Wisconsin. Yes, she was pregnant! She was only in her first trimester and the restless seven were welcomed and cherished once again at our grandparent's home. It was just a temporary arrangement, PART TWO of The Homeless Upenleaves, while waiting for a large-enough house to become available at the closest military base. It turned out to be a three month wait. During those three months, many timeless memories were forged. Grandma Rachael would serve lunch made-to-order. Every day my mom would stipulate, "Mother, just make some sandwiches. These kids will eat whatever you make them." But every day Grandma Rachael would ask each and every one of us what kind of a sandwich we wanted . . . and made it just how we liked it.

Other than the sleeping arrangements, the house and surroundings had great appeal for most of us kids. There was a magnificent park within a half mile of our grandparent's house. It had a shimmering lake with plenty of wild ducks and geese that had an uncanny ability to sniff out the kids with the snacks. If you tried to pretend there were no pretzels or peanut butter crackers in your pocket you quickly became the center of attention.

The sound of ducks and geese honking and quacking to the tune of "c'mon chump, we know you got the goodies," made everyone at the park stop, stare and say to themselves, *"gee, I wonder how this is going to end?"*

One time, a boy was accosted by geese, so he stuffed the rest of his Dolly Madison mini donuts into his mouth, shook out the package, then threw his arms into the air signifying "NO MAS!" An eerie silence was followed by a spattering of applause. The fiery fowl ambled away as the on-lookers mumbled words of admiration. After swallowing the last morsels of Dolly Madison goodness his first step was *squirshhh,* right in the middle of a pile of goose poop.

Back at our grandparent's house, on the other side of the back yard chain-linked fence was a fantastic sledding hill that led right to the elementary school parking lot. The fantasy of sledding to school with books in a pillow case was a daily occurrence.

**Excursions from School**

The first day at another new school had arrived and all the elementary schoolers had to do was walk down the street one block, turn right, walk the sidewalk at the bottom of the hill (or cut across the parking lot) and presto! When the final bell sounded, reverse the direction. Brett Favre could throw a football from grandpa's backyard and nail the principle as he greeted the children entering the school (another fantasy).

Like other times before, our family had to pack it up and move in the middle of a school year. Making new friends was almost effortless for Donna, Denise, Steve and Phil. For Fred and Cindy it was easier said than done. Fred and Cindy were more inhibited than normal. Perhaps that was a blessing in disguise, because the joy of making and having a new friend was almost always eclipsed by the heartache of having to desert him or her when it came time to do the Upenleave shuffle . . . again.

Philip(6) was in first grade and while he was already familiar with the process of hopping into a new school mid-year, this would be the first time he actually had to walk. Donna and Fred were in middle school which was an entirely different building. Cindy, Denise, Steve and Phil would just walk to the corner, then take the sidewalk down and around to the elementary school.

By all rights Philip should have been escorted home after school, so when the restless seven were all present or accounted for in Grandpa's front yard, except Philip, mother became curious. "Steven, why didn't you walk home with Philip?" she inquired.

"I looked for him, but I couldn't find him. I figured he already started walking," was Steve's reply.

"Oh dear. Well, you and Fred will have to go back."

"Hey Look!" Denise butted in, pointing to a bus rolling by.

There in one of the back seats with hands clawing at the window and tears beginning to stream was Philip, becoming more panicky each second that the bus shifted gears and picked up speed. It was apparent that his decision to take the bus home wasn't working out too well at the moment. Everyone in the yard stood there and watched him disappear in a state of shock and bewilderment, and ultimately . . . helplessness.

The second the bus was out of view, mom was saturated with a barrage of questions and assertions. Her protective instincts were suddenly, seriously, challenged.

"Where's he going?"

"What was he thinking?"

"He's bawling!"

"No wonder I couldn't find him."

"Quiet, please!" Mother firmly requested, "I need to think."

"Let's go down to the school and talk to the people in the office." Grandma Rachael advised.

"Ok. You don't think we should follow the bus, Mom?" Marcia replied to grandma.

"With what? Wilson (grandpa) has the car."

"Right. Let me get my sweater."

Donna and Fred were instructed to wait in the front yard. In case the bus came back around they were to wave it down, if necessary.

About fifteen minutes later, grandma and mom returned to a yard full of kids brimming with anxiety. Donna was the first to get their attention. "Did they call the bus driver?"

Mom shook her head. "The buses don't have radios."

"Sooooo, what do we do?" Fred wanted to know.

"Well, pretty much . . . nothing." Mom sighed.

Tense minutes ensued, then about thirty minutes later an empty bus squeaked to a stop.
Philip bounced out with a sheepish grin. Mom thanked the bus driver while Phil was pampered a little then swamped with a barrage of questions himself. Of course, he was teased about it forever.


## Malicious Contraption

It was a cool, fall morning. On this particular day the distant clouds were ominous. While mother was prepping the younger children for school, grandma was telling everyone about the impending weather. There was a storm coming towards us that would bring high winds and heavy rainfall.

Donna and Fred had already started walking, since middle school had an earlier start than elementary school.

Grandma Rachael scanned the children and noticed Cindy (9), the eldest of this bunch, was particularly nervous about the weather.

"I don't think I want to go to school today, Mom." Cindy pouted.

"Oh really, mom quipped, and why not young lady?"

"I don't wanna get wet." she whined.

"Oh, Cynthia Louise!" mom frowned.

Grandma Rachael left the room then returned with an umbrella. "Why don't you take my umbrella to school with you, Cynthia. If it's raining when school is dismissed this will keep you dry." Cindy beamed at the thought of being trusted with grandma's umbrella. She held it up like a championship trophy for all of her siblings to see.

"Thank you, grandma! I'll take good care of it."

"Yes. I know, dear. Bring it home with you, rain or shine, Ok?"

"Ok."

Mom showed Cindy how to operate it then let her try.   "Are you ready to go, little missy?" Mother smiled.

"Come on, Mary Poppins," Steve taunted. "You're gonna make us late!"

Mom gave everyone a hug and scooted us along our way.

Around mid-day the storm swept into the area. The winds and rain were intermittent, but as luck would have it, Mother Nature kicked it up a notch just before the school bell rang. Grandma and mom were anxious to see how Cindy would perform. They were worried about the strength of the wind at the moment.

Fortunately, they were able to watch the children exit the school from the kitchen window.

Cindy stepped out of the school and looked for any of us hanging around.

It was raining too hard to tell. With this nasty weather upon them, everyone was covered up by a raincoat or an umbrella. "Well, here goes." She told herself as she opened the umbrella.

It opened with such ferocity she had to squeeze with all her might to keep it from being ripped away.

Wasting no time, she moved at a swift pace on the sidewalk. The wind was indeed forceful, so she held on to the curved handle with both hands. She turned right and was walking at the bottom of the grassy hill when a mighty gust swept under the umbrella and lifted it a foot. Cindy clamped down with both hands as the umbrella climbed another foot and wasn't finished yet. Cindy realized that she was three feet off the ground and headed for the busy street.

If she let go, she would be safe, but Grandma's umbrella would fly away and Grandma would never trust her again.

She couldn't let go. She wanted grandma to be proud of her. She would hold on until the wind died. Surely it would die any second. In the next few seconds, she climbed higher yet.

Now Cindy was scared.

She began kicking her feet, hoping that the furious scissor maneuver would somehow counteract the force of the wind, permitting the umbrella to descend slowly and gently.

What it actually did was enhance the hilarity mom and grandma were engulfed in while witnessing this episode from grandma's kitchen window.

Cindy was not letting go and not looking at all. She was headed for the street, kicking and praying. If she had been looking, she would have noticed that all the cars had stopped to admire her acrobatic demonstration.

Regardless, her prayers were answered about ten feet from the street. Cynthia Poppins executed a ham-fisted, crash landing that made the spectators cringe.

Cindy was too embarrassed and upset to stay still. She picked herself up and sprinted up the hill. At the top of the hill, she slowed down, noticing the umbrella was folded all the way up. It was broken! What else could go wrong today! She became a public spectacle, was nearly killed, drenched and ruined her grandma's umbrella. Tears were forming and by the time she got to our grandparents' house they were streaming.

Rachael and Marcia were waiting for her at the kitchen door  Cindy was clearly distressed as she lifted the umbrella. "I'm sorry, I . . . sniffle . . . broke your um . . . snort . . . umbrella, Grandma."

"Awwww, you didn't break it, Cynthia." Grandma reassured. "We just need to pull it back down again, that's all."

Did she hear her right? The umbrella wasn't broken?
Well alrighty then! Cindy finally looked up at the women with a hint of relief in her eyes. In fact, she actually felt a sense of pride for returning with the damned malicious contraption.

She expected to see sympathetic eyes looking down on her, but instead, what she thought she saw was something joyful. Yes. She was sure of it!
Her mother and grandmother were smirking as if they were trying to hold back laughter. Their eyes appeared to be glistening with delight!
*What the . . . ????*

Had they not seen the perilous, near catastrophe that took place right behind grandma's back yard?

Well, she had had enough torment today to last her a lifetime, so she stomped her way to the bedroom for some dry clothes.

Many years passed before Cindy mustered the courage to open another one of those malicious contraptions. She was reminded of them constantly because we teased her about it forever!!

## Playing with the Big Boys

There is a single element which nearly every individual in this book has vivid memories of. The measure of snowfall on the ground turned all of Monona, Wisconsin into a playground. Before that first winter in Wisconsin snow was just something we watched actors and animations romp around in. Now it was our turn!

Snowball fights and snow angels quickly progressed into the desire to go sledding on the hill behind grandpa's house. Sleds were acquired that were made of wooden slats on metal runners with a pivoting handle for steering. They were crude, even for the late 1960s, but do you think that was going to deter us?

There were three sleds among the five sledding virgins that ventured across the fence and over to the hill next to the elementary school. They each took turns speeding down the 30 degree embankment and maneuvering through the playground equipment in back of the elementary school. It was real exhilarating stuff for a bunch of Air Force brats who were used to beaches and deserts.

But there was something going on in the distance, further behind the elementary school that diminished their merriment. The local kids had built a ramp, placed it at the top of a hill in an area adjacent to a patch of dense woods.

They could tell from where they were standing that the speed of the sleds coming off of that ramp and thrusting into those woods was at least 5 times greater than their comparatively lame experience.

"Does anybody want to see what's going on over there?" Donna (12) inquired, confident that she would have a good following. She was right. Steve (7) and Denise (8) championed the proposal. Fred and Cindy went along out of sheer anticipation.

As they stood next to the ramp watching the local boys and a few older girls catapult downhill, and disappear, into the woods screaming and laughing, it gave the sledding rookies an immediate, involuntary shot of adrenaline.

"That's the craziest shit I've ever seen!" Steve roused.
"Are you hungry for a bar of soap?" Donna warned. "No more foul language or Mom will hear about it."
Steve gave her a defiant "hmpff" and made his way to the steps of the ramp. Denise jumped ahead of him and got in line first.

Donna, Fred and Cindy, the oldest of the rookies, apparently were not the bravest of the rookies.

"I don't think it's such a good idea, guys." Fred deduced. "We're not very good at this stuff yet."
"How do think you get good?" Denise argued.

54

"Ahhh, let em go, Donna concurred. It won't kill them."

"The trees might!" Cindy chimed.

"That's way too fast for us." Fred warned.

Donna was watching the two thrill seekers like a mother hen as they got closer to the steps of the ramp. Perhaps she was expecting one or both of them to chicken out?

The locals had rope or twine tied to the front rail of their sleds so they could sling it over their backs as they climbed the steps to the top of the ramp. "Make sure you hold on tight!" Donna yelled as Denise suddenly realized there was nobody in front of her. The grip of fear squeezed her throat. She tried to swallow, but it was as dry as the El Paso desert.

By that time Donna and the other two cowardly rookies were waiting half-way down the hill to get a good vantage point of the two daredevils as they zipped into the treacherous woods.

"You goin' or what, Denise?" Steve badgered. Denise glanced back at the impatient locals waiting in line behind her.

"Don't rush me, man! First timer here!" she declared to the crowd.

After a sprinkle of murmurs, she turned and made her way to the top of the ramp, fumbling with her sled the entire way. At the top she took a deep breath. "here I go!" she called out, and away she went – down the ramp and down the hill.

Denise's screams were blood curdling but brief. In seconds she had disappeared into the woods and the world was quiet.

Then her laughter broke the silence.

Steve was at the top of the ramp, questioning his judgment, looking back at the smirking locals and realizing it was way too late to chicken out now. Especially since Denise just went for it.

He eased onto his sled and tried to drag his hands and feet to slow the momentum . . . wooosh!! The sled took off like a Banshee! Denise was half-way through the run and had slowed to approximately 20 mph. After the first sharp turn on the tightly packed and well cut channel through the woods, she learned to hold her legs firmly together and try to keep the sled in the middle. Taking the curves without letting your feet swing out was the key to a painless trip.

Steve was approaching the woods and if you thought Denise's screams were insufferable, you should have heard his. His screams were higher pitched, and they persisted for what seemed like the entire run. He tried to decelerate by dragging his toes. Big mistake! The sled started swerving wildly and was right on the edge of the channel. His feet swung out and WAP! They bounced off of a tree, creating more erratic movement. He wrangled the rickety sled for control and wasn't feeling any pain . . . just yet. There was too much adrenaline coursing through his body.

The first sharp curve almost did him in, but he fought it with all his might and kept his legs straight the rest of the run, barely missing a few more tree trunks.

Denise was waiting for him on the other side of the woods with a major smile and busload of enthusiasm.
"That was awesome, wasn't it? Let's go again! Are you gonna go again? Wow! That was like a roller coaster on ice!"

Steve couldn't get a word in edgewise, but it didn't matter. He was too stunned to say anything.

In his seven years of existence, that was the scariest shit he had ever attempted. He simply shook his head and walked past Denise like a useless zombie.
"You didn't like it, did you? You friggin wussy!" Denise teased. "I'm going down again. That was cool!"

They tramped through the snow together and joined the other three. Steve surrendered his sled at once and Denise talked Donna and Fred into giving it a go. Cindy was an adamant coward and Steve was starting to limp a little. He plopped down in a nice safe spot to watch the action and rub his foot.

Denise was the only one to go down more than once. It was an exhilarating yet terrifying experience and they were no longer sledding virgins!

# Grandma Rachael in Charge

**Sun Prairie, Wisconsin - 1969**

Dad was still in Okinawa, but we finally got moved into a house in Sun Prairie next to the Army National Guard, which was roughly two hours from Monona.

With father being overseas and mom on the verge of augmenting her family unit . . . again, Grandma Rachael cheerfully volunteered to step in as head of the household leading up to the birth of Christopher on July 22nd 1969. Grandma Rachael was a quiet, efficient lady who aged gracefully and demonstrated a calm, humanitarian outlook. On this particular afternoon, however, grandma's ability to remain poised was being tested. She was experiencing the full, robust, flavor of a woman raising seven children single-handedly.

She had just finished vacuuming the living and dining room areas and had started to gather the dirty laundry when four year-old Teresa slunk up to her. Teresa was a morning pre-schooler, so she had the distinct benefit of one-on-one pestering in the afternoon while all the other kids were in school.

"Gama, I don't want to play outside no more." Teresa moped with tears running down her cheeks.

"What's wrong, sweetheart?" grandma soothed, while she wiped Teresa's cheeks with the bottom of her apron.

"That boy. We was having fun and, and then all he wants to do is wrestle! I don't want to wrestle, gama."

"Did you tell him so?"

"Yes. Then he called me names."

"Why don't you find someone else to play with, dear?"

"I tried, gama! He keeps bugging me!" Grandma shook her head as she stepped into the kitchen. Teresa followed, eagerly awaiting her sage advice. Grandma handed Teresa a cup of water and Teresa gulped it down. She filled it up again but this time Teresa refused it. "Thank you, Gama, I not thirsty no more.

"Go ahead and take it with you outside, sweetie. If that boy keeps bugging you, pour it on him."

Teresa shrugged. "Ok"

Minutes later, Teresa returned with an empty cup and Cheshire grin.

"How did it go?" Grandma pried.

"It worked! When he bugged me I poured it on his hair!"

Grandma snickered. She was impressed with Teresa's spunk.

"I made his shirt wet too. Then . . . his pants getted wet and he ran home."

Teresa joined the giggle-fest as Grandma Rachael decided it was time for lunch.

**Karma?**

A few days later, Teresa was in her morning pre-school class. The teacher set up an easel and white cardboard for each child and quickly got their attention.

"Ok children, we have a special project in store, the teacher smiled. We are all going to be artists today!"

Oooohhhhs and aaaahhhhhs filled the room and the children grew restless.

"Everyone will paint a picture of you and your family doing something that makes you happy!"
The children bristled with excitement as they were placed in front of an easel and given finger paints.

Teresa only thought about it for a few seconds then got down to painting her entire family on a picnic.

The teacher was making her rounds between them when she glanced upon Teresa's drawing she started counting the stick figures and laughed quietly.

"You're going to need another board for your family," she teased.

"Ummm, I think I'll fit them here, Miss Blake." Teresa assured her.

"Very good, Teresa."
The little girl next to Teresa stepped back to admire Teresa's work.

"Nice picnic," she complimented. "Do you live at a circus, like Dumbo?"

"No, silly, we're castlelic." Teresa bragged.

"Ok, well, do you want to help me paint mine?"

"No way!"

"It's ok, I don't mind."

"I don't think I should." Teresa rebuffed.

"But I want you to help me! Right now!" The little girl stomped.

Teresa dipped her fingers in the blue paint and created some clouds at the top of the little girl's board.

"Wow! I didn't think of that. Can you make a horsy?"

There was something that looked like a house and some straight green lines that were supposed to be grass, but no people yet. Teresa sized it up and weighed her options.

"What color?"

"Yellow!" the girl insisted.

"Just what do you think you are doing, Teresa?" Miss Blake asked sharply.

The little girl jerked like a startled skunk. Teresa gazed back at Miss Blake and squinted.

"A horsy . . . should I put it there . . . or there?"

Before she could straighten her pointing finger, Miss Blake was wiping Teresa's hands clean with a rag.

"You march right over and stand in that corner little missy! We are not to draw on our neighbors art work."

"But, but, she told me to."

"No buts. Just go!"

Teresa slogged over to the corner.

If it weren't for her sudden wave of hatred toward her stupid teacher she would have cried loud enough for the entire school to hear. She stood with her face in the corner, stewing, sneaking peaks at the little girl, who was painting merrily, for what seemed like an hour. Finally the stupid teacher tapped her on the shoulder.

"You may finish your own art work, Teresa." Teresa pivoted slowly around to reveal the streaks on her cheeks and the significant splotch of wetness on the front of her pants.

"Oh, my goodness," Miss Blake mumbled. "Come with me." She took Teresa's hand and walked her to the office.

All the kids except Chris with grandma, grandpa, and Aunt Jeanine.

# Georgia Peaches

## Warner Robbins, Georgia - 1970

When dad returned from Okinawa, his final duty
station was Warner Robbins AFB, Georgia. Mom
and dad found a nice, ranch-style, brick house.
There was a hideous six-foot deep, ten-foot wide,
ditch abutting our back yard. If we traversed the
ditch and walked across a 100 yard field, we were
at our elementary school. The high school was
another half- mile further.

The peach orchards were a favorite destination at
this duty station. It was pick them yourself and
pay by the bushel. Understandably, it didn't take
long for our family to collect a bushel of peaches.
We took our sweet time and sampled plenty of the
wares before the orchard owners begged us to
leave.

## Bonzo

A few weeks into getting settled in, a docile knock
at the kitchen door interrupted mom's dinner
preparation. It was after 4:00 P.M. Us kids were
doing homework or playing outside. She opened it
and saw nothing but the school across the field.
She closed the door and wondered if she needed to
take a break. *Naaaa, back to the chopping of
vegetables*!

Then the subtle knock came again. She wiped her
hands on the apron Donna made in school three
years ago.

Opening the door slowly, a voice got her attention. She peered down at the ground to view a disheveled little boy with a worried look on his face.

"Um, scuse me maam', um, do you have a nanner for Bonzo?"

Now mother had undoubtedly heard a lot of crazy gibberish from the likes of her own tikes, but for some reason this set her off. She laughed so hard, we kids who were doing homework scurried into the kitchen just to satisfy our curiosities. Mom took some deep breaths and managed to scale the hysterics down to snickers. "I'm so sorry, little boy. Oh, goodness gracious. What is your name?"

"My name is Bobby. Do you have a . . .
Mom cut him off with a hand gesture and fought the urge to laugh her ass off again.

"So, let me get this straight, Bobby. You have a friend or brother? Named Bonzo?" Mom said with a restrained chuckle.

"Sorta . . . not really." Bobby pandered.

He backed up and beckoned mom outside. She acquiesced and Bobby pointed up to the sky.

"That's Bonzo up there."

*"Is this boy out of his mind? What on earth is going on here?"* Mom wondered.

The sky was partly cloudy but otherwise vacant of anybody doing something outrageous.

There were telephone lines along the street and a monkey sitting on one of the telephone poles, but no sign of anyone who . . . *what the hell is a monkey doing up on that telephone pole?*
With wide eyes and mouth agape she addressed Bobby. "That's Bonzo! Right?"

"Yaaaa! He won't come down for nothin' but a nanner!"

Marcia slapped her forehead and didn't bother to restrain the amusement she felt.

"Donna, would you bring me one of those bananas on the kitchen counter?"

Donna gladly complied. Marcia handed the banana to Bobby. He thanked her and hurried over to telephone pole as Marcia's kids and some neighborhood kids congregated.

Bobby peeled the banana, took a healthy bite and yelled up to the skies. "Here, Bonzo!" "Got you a nanner!"

That's all it took. Bonzo, the spider monkey, scurried down that pole and leaped up into Bobby's arms for some delish, nutrish, banana. Marcia had a smile on her face the rest of the evening and the kids desperately wanted a pet monkey!

## Youth Group Track Meet

At the end of the school year there was an annual track meet. It was a track and field competition between neighboring youth groups.

All of us physically able-bodied children except Fred were coerced by Donna to take part.
It was a rare day when Fred got involved in any sports activity. He had not outgrown his clumsiness and got no enjoyment out of any sport.

The youth group met at the high school track on a brisk Saturday morning and dad was at the ready with his 8mm camera.

Everyone got a large, black and gold jersey with a number on it. Donna's was the right length. She had legs that grew out of her armpits. Cindy, Denise and Steve looked like go-go dancers and Phil . . . well, he looked liked someone's athletic grandma in running shoes. Seriously, that shirt hit him at mid-calf.

They started with the youngest age group. Phil was running the 100 yard dash.

At the starting gun, Phil had a respectable chance, but within 5 seconds, dad was faced with the dilemma of recording the five boys in the lead, pushing their limits or Grandma Phil churning and burning 20 yards behind them. He filmed Phil most of the way then panned the camera on the finish line as the other boys approached it.

It was a close race. Three boys finished within milliseconds of each other. Then two more crossed one second apart. Then Phil came . . . *any second now . . . ok, where the hell is he*? Dad panned the camera back a little and there he was! Using every ounce of pride he could muster to lope across that finish line. At least he was smiling. Steve could not stop laughing, but Phil got the last laugh when Steve's race was almost a carbon copy. Fred was looking like a genius about now.

Cindy and Denise ran the same race. In typical fashion, they battled each other for distant last place. Who got the not-last-place victory? Let's check the replay, Dad? Ohhh! Denise edged Cindy with an elbow!

Donna had the lead in her race, but was overtaken at the finish line by a speedster with miniscule leg-length.

We all competed in a couple more events. Donna finished strong in them as well. The rest of us couldn't wait for the damn thing to end!

When the track meet finally wound down and everyone, with the exception of Donna, was licking their wounds and rejuvenating their pride, dad praised all of us and declared, "This was fun! I can't wait to watch it again after I get this film developed."

Yes, the embarrassment of the Warner Robbins track meet was replicated on 8mm at least once a year, more frequently if any relatives came to visit.

## The Perfect Lair - 1971

Our next-door neighbor in Warner Robbins had only one child, a six year old daughter named Kim. Teresa (5) and Kim played together often.

Kim shared her many dolls with Teresa, they played house and other kids games, like, pretending to be doctors. When they played doctors, Phil (9) was usually invited into the surgery room. Doctors were men in 1971.

The next door neighbors on the opposite side had two girls, Terry and Tanya. Tanya was Donna's age while Terry was two years older.

By now, you shouldn't be shocked at the proposition of Donna (14) hanging out with her friend's seventeen year-old sister. However, with the information we have gathered in Donna's previous exploits, we can be pretty sure of two things:
A. There will be mischief.
B. Boys will be involved.

Harmless mischief during summer vacation makes the day fun and memorable. Terry's idea of fun was walking to a record shop just outside the base.

Terry had a driver's license, but no vehicle. This was no ordinary record shop. There were beads hanging in the doorways, incense burning and a small collection of bongs and pipes for the smoking of marijuana.

Most of the time they would just browse and flirt with the cute guy who wore the rose-colored John Lennon glasses, but on occasion Terry would make a purchase. An LP, vinyl, man!

At dusk all the kids in the neighborhood would flock to the huge vacant lot across the street where all the sports activities went down.
A football was tossed around until someone got thumped in the face indicating that it was dark enough for the real game to commence. The game of choice was spotlight, a night-time version of hide and seek. The seeker tries to spot the hiders with a flashlight before they make it back to home base.

Terry, Donna and Tanya would usually join the fray, but some nights they just needed some privacy (with a scrupulous selection of cute boys, of course).
Since there was nobody among them whose parents were frequently out of the house, they were forced to improvise in order to commandeer a comfy lair. On this particular night they were joined by Chad and Joshua.

Before they got out of the neighborhood, Terry caught up to them and hollered from behind.

"Hey, Tanya! Where are you guys going to?"
Terry was hoping she could tag along, but Tanya
wasn't too keen on that idea. Tanya had been
listening in English class that week and her reply
was terse.

"We aren't sure where we're going, Terry . . .
and don't end your sentences with a preposition."

"Ok, well . . . Where are you guys going to,
bitch?"

They strolled out of our neighborhood, without
Terry, and were cutting across a weed infested lot
where a double-wide R.V. was parked. Chad
walked over to the R.V. like he was delivering a
pizza . . . and opened the door.

"No way!" Chad exclaimed, surprised that
he had access to a veritable pie wagon! "Hello!!
Anybody home?"

The sound of crickets chirping filled the night air.

Joshua was the son of a police officer. He wasn't
too keen about trespassing. "It's not legal for us to
go in there, bro."

"Ahhh, we won't stay long. Let's just check it
out." Chad suggested.

The chicks concurred so everyone piled in, making
themselves at home for a few minutes.
When the cop's son got nervous they hit the trail
again. This routine went on for a couple of weeks.
Every other night, instead of playing spotlight they
would walk to the R.V.

Needless to say, the group of kids became more and more comfortable with their latest and grooviest hideout. Sometimes Chad would fire up a doobie and pass it around. They always locked the door from the inside yet nobody ever disturbed them.

Of course, just when the young intruders started acting like it was 'their' place a forceful knock on the door jolted them to reality. They were deer in headlights, holding their breath.

"Who's in there!" A peeved man yelled. He shook the handle then knocked again.

"I heard you talking in there. I'm giving ya ten seconds to get the hell out!"

The cop's son took a quick peek out of the corner of a window. The man was scanning the windows for signs of life.

"Let's get out of here." He whispered.

"Is he gone?" Donna asked.

"No. he's still there . . . wait! He's leaving. He's walking back to that house over there."

"I have to use the restroom," Tanya squirmed.

"Really, Tanya? You can't hold it for five minutes?" Chad harassed her.

"What bathroom can we get to in five minutes?" she countered.

"Make it quick, chick. We gotta split." Tanya made her way to the toilet while Joshua stayed on the lookout.

"Holy crap! There's a cop car. Please keep moving, keep moving . . . No! He stopped.

I can't get caught in here. My Dad will torture me then send me to military school."

Joshua made a bee-line for the door and wisely, the others followed. Chad whispered through the bathroom door before he high-tailed it.

"Lock the door and stay quiet, Tanya."

"What for?" Tanya whispered back.

No answer, he was gone.

Joshua peeked around the door, saw it was all clear, and bolted for the house opposite where the peeved man lived. The others were right on his tail. It was a clean getaway. They were all smiles when they reached the back side of the adjacent house.

In the meantime, the police officer was escorted to the R. V. by the peeved man, who still appeared to be peeved. The officer turned the door handle and opened the door.

"Stay here, sir. I'll be right back." The policeman instructed.

The cop walked slowly through the aisle, looking for clues; remnants the perps had left behind. All he found was a coke can with ashes on top. He recognized the smell of tobacco and the faint smell of marijuana in the air. Then he sauntered to the bathroom door. Funny, it was locked.

*Why would they lock the bathroom from the inside yet leave the front door unlocked?* The officer reasoned. It did not seem logical.

"Who's in there?" He demanded as he pounded his fist on the flimsy particle board.

Tanya was shaking like she was on a naked polar expedition. But she didn't make a sound.

Somewhat satisfied or realizing that there was nothing he could do, the cop gave up and left the R.V. with the coke can.

"They were just in there, I'm tellin' ya," the peeved man insisted.

"There's no damage or signs of criminal behavior, sir  Why wasn't it locked?"

"The owner wants me to air it out, but he doesn't want me to have the keys."

"I see. Well, I suggest you put a no trespassing sign up somewhere, ok? Have a good night."

As the police car rolled away, the peeved man tromped back to his house and the four teens reveled with quiet high-fives.

As they were sneaking back to the R.V. to collect Tanya, a thunderous, extensive fart stopped them in their tracks. While they struggled to remain silent, Tanya moaned with sheer ecstasy. Now they had to run back behind the house because they couldn't stop laughing.

Cool heads finally prevailed and Joshua was chosen to retrieve Tanya. When he entered the R.V. she was almost at the door herself.

"God, that was gross, Tanya." Joshua scolded.

"Whatever," she defended, "I had to hold that mess so long I thought my eyes were gonna pop out, hit the door, and give me away."

"Yeah, I gotta give you a high five for that. Wait . . . did you wash?"

"Of course I did, you butt. You owe me big time. I thought your dad was gonna break that door down."

"What? That was my dad? Holy shit!"

The trespassers walked home and laughed about the close call and Tanya's gas the entire way. A pact was made to keep the lid on it so Joshua could remain in the public school with them.

## Tails of Fury

Daytime activities among the middle children varied depending on their mood and the weather. Catching lizards in the ditch behind the house was extremely popular during the summer, primarily because of a defense mechanism that the lizards used. It was no easy task to capture one of the speedy reptiles. They would blitz from one object to the next, going forward as soon as they felt you move. But if you worked together as a team, trapping a lizard was possible.

Denise (11), Steve and Phil became expert lizard trappers in that deep clay ditch. Denise clamped down on her very first lizard and boasted, "I got him!"

She pinched him to the ground with her thumb and forefinger while the lizard thrashed to and fro. Then the lizard ejected it's tail, which continued to thrash.

"What the . . . ?" Denise freaked out and abruptly let it go.

They gawked for an excessive amount of time considering it was . . . a lizard tail.

The rite would recur every time they captured a lizard and based on their levels of fascination, amount of free time, and sheer determination they may have set the world record for number of lizards captured, then released without its tail.

## Brush your Hair!

At some point that summer mother threatened to get Cindy (12) and Denise a perm if they didn't start brushing their hair more frequently.

I guess they didn't take her seriously until one afternoon mom put Donna in charge, ordered her ratty-haired daughters into the station wagon and took them to the military hair salon.

As the disgruntled pair were having their heads shampooed, a tick was discovered in Denise's scalp. The tick was easily extracted but it put the kibosh on Denise's perm.

"Oh, man, that's too bad, smirked Denise. I guess I'll just get a trim."

"What? Cindy protested. That's not fair!"

"How was I supposed to know I had a tick in my head?"

"By brushing it!" mom trumped.

Mom had the solution in mind already, so when it was all said and done, she enjoyed a quiet drive home with two surly but silent teenagers: one with a perm one with a pixie.

Denise found comfort in the scores of stocking caps saved from the previous winter. She had to carry one of dad's handkerchiefs to wipe the sweat from her face, but she thought it was a fair tradeoff.

Denise  Teresa  Donna

## Retirement

Leaving Georgia was inevitable and the time was near. Don was quickly approaching his twenty year mark in the Air Force and had already made the decision to try the civilian life.

The next door neighbor gave Don and Marcia the name and number of his brother who resided in Hicktown, Missouri.

That wasn't the name of the town, but it might as well have been. The population was just over 200. 185 of them were farmers.

The neighbor's brother lived about a half mile from a large, vacant farmhouse that happened to be for rent. Don's parents and most of his siblings resided in Missouri.
Having his family nearby was appealing and Don grew up in a self-sufficient household so he knew the value of raising children in a farm-like setting. It was too good to be true.

About a month before the departure, Steve, Phil and Teresa were walking in the field behind their house, just exploring on a nice day. Teresa abruptly shhh'ed Steve and proclaimed. "I heard something."
        "I didn't hear anything," Steve quipped.
        "Uhh, that's because you were too busy babbling." Teresa informed him.

Then a high pitched whimper echoed with a metallic resonance. The kids were next to a ditch. The ditch was fortified with stainless steel drainage tubes.

They ran to the nearest tube and discovered a cute, miserable puppy who was trying to tell the world that he was wet, hungry and apparently homeless. There was no collar on him, so he wasn't claimed and they were no where near any houses.

They took turns holding him as they tromped back home. He was black and tan with fluffy hair, a mix of German Sheppard and Husky. They named him Fluffy.

Marcia put up an insignificant amount of resistance to the prospect of keeping the puppy.

"We'll keep him until someone comes and claims him." she cautioned. "Don't get too attached to him."

It wasn't until days before the move that a distant neighbor boy straggled into their yard and exclaimed,

"Hey, that's our puppy! His name is Rover. Here Rover!"

Marcia thought, "*well, he was definitely roving when the kids found him . . . but . . . Fluffy already loved the kids and the kids were very fond of him*". . . so she told the boy to piss off and that was the end of that.

# A Different Life

## Hicktown, Missouri - 1971

Dad drove the station wagon with Donna, Fred, Cindy and Denise from Warner Robbins to Hick Town, Missouri. Fluffy was the guest of honor who, surprisingly, did not mind being caged for the entire trip. Well, there was the initial nervousness of the first car ride, the result of which was a healthy vomiting, but after that he was just glad to be along for the trip. It was a fairly uneventful fourteen hour drive.

Mom, Steve, Phil, Teresa and Christopher had the privilege of flying to their new destination. Their flight was also uneventful, with the exception of Phil spilling his drink and creating Teresa's infamous 'peed my pants' look.

Their new home wasn't exactly new. In fact, it had been standing for over a century. The living and dining rooms were spacious, as was the kitchen. There was a bedroom downstairs and two adjoining bedrooms upstairs. There was no basement, just a small, dank cellar with a dirt floor.

When mother and the girls discovered that there was one small bathroom with a toilet and a tub (no shower), a rebellious uprising ensued. How dad managed to weasel his way out of that female firestorm is anyone's guess. But we stayed in that farmhouse for nearly ten years, a lifetime compared to our previous homes.

The area surrounding our house was all Missouri River bottom farm land. Hiller's Creek, a tributary of the Missouri River, ran North and South about 100 yards from the farmhouse.

There was a 100 x 50 yard field on the East side of the creek that became the Multi-purpose Event Center. It was bordered by a pig pen to the North and the gravel road to the South. That field hosted football, softball, cork ball and soccer games (when the wind wasn't blowing from the North). There were campouts, cookouts, fireworks and it eventually graduated to a grazing/birthing area for the horses we raised.

A softball game with cousins at the Multi-purpose Event Center

Directly North of the farmhouse was an open one-car garage that dad used for storing equipment, tools and hardware. Right next to that was a larger, taller garage which the landlord used to store and maintain his farm equipment. On the North end of the pig pen was a substantial barn for the pigs, our horses and storing hay.

The back (North side) of the farmhouse and two garages

One of the eye sores, besides the farmhouse itself, was the chicken coop which was only fifty feet Northwest of the house. The majority vote was to tear it down and burn it, but dad vetoed the hostile reaction and put that chicken coop to good use within the first three years. Fresh eggs and fried chicken on Sundays turned out to be a damn good argument for putting up with the stench. We raised practically every tame bird known to mankind, including peacocks.

Rabbits were the first animals that dad surprised us with. That would become an annoying habit of his.

It's quite possible that a couple of us kids acquired a gambling habit at this stage of our lives.
We were constantly placing wagers for chores or deeds with each other on the next animal dad would haul home in the back of his pickup.

There were about ten hutches lined up under the trees close to the creek that housed up to forty rabbits. The ornery ones that didn't like roommates usually got butchered first.

When Cindy first witnessed a rabbit butchering in the back yard, it put the kibosh on her meat and potatoes suppers. She didn't go strictly veggie, but the meat had to be distinctly white for her to dine on it.
It was a drastic change from the Air Force bases that our crew had grown use to. We were country folk now. Yeeehaaaaaw!

## Attitude Checks

All kidding aside, it was a difficult adjustment to make (especially for the oldest kids). The stark contrast between our Air Force lives and our Hicktown life was something to be reckoned with.

Fred wasn't reckoning with it successfully. His outlook on the country lifestyle was the most pessimistic of our entire gang.
He was in high school and pretty much set in the ways of an Air Force brat. Farm labor was beneath him. His goal was to get the hell out of . . . hell. Soon was not soon enough.

There were a few girls in town that were around his age and Fred was skinny, but handsome. He merely lacked the social skills and the ambition to make an impression.

Donna's situation was no different. Her adjustment to the new lifestyle was simply much more positive than her brother's. She had grown into an attractive girl and got plenty of attention wherever she went.

You have read about some of her previous exploits, so I don't have to tell you that her social skills came naturally, which lead to her plethora of friends near and far. Being the oldest of eight and the most responsible of the elders turned out to be more of a curse than a blessing for Donna. She willingly and admirably took on the role of parent when both mom and dad took full-time jobs, but whenever the opportunity emerged she made her escape to the city or called her new friend, Mark, who lived five miles west along the gravel road. Mark would zip over to the farmhouse anytime Donna wanted to take a motorcycle ride. Basically, when she wasn't in charge of the pack, she was not stuck at the farmhouse.

Cindy actually made friends with Mark's younger brother. He liked her so much that on Valentines Day he showered her with an exquisite baby chicken. She loved it.

## Chicken Pluckin'

Dad had already gotten a banny rooster and a half-dozen chickens to occupy the coop, so when Cindy's chick grew up it fit right in.
She fed her pet chicken daily and played with it regularly. Cindy's chicken would mature into a feisty defender that everyone tried to avoid.

All of us kids took turns collecting eggs from the adult chickens. Everyone got pecked a time or seven.

Of course, some of the eggs were left alone so the chickens could multiply.

Somehow, dad knew which chickens weren't producing many eggs and they were selected for the very first chicken pluckin' contest. That's right, dad held up a crisp five dollar bill and promised it to the person who could pluck their chicken the fastest.

Mom was lobbying against killing the chickens in front of the girls, but dad simply had no choice.

We were already lined up in the back yard and it was getting late. He pulled the first victim out of a cage by its legs smacked it down on a wooden barrel and came down with a machete. Instant decapitation!

With speed and accuracy he tossed the head in a five gallon bucket and flung the chicken to the ground.

Among the five kids waiting to pluck a chicken (Donna, Teresa and Chris were MIA), there wasn't a single ex Air Force brat whose jaw wasn't hanging below his/her neck. Phil had to get a closer look at the headless chicken flopping wildly and spraying blood everywhere. No wonder dad was in his filthy overalls. He could have at least given us a heads up on the proper attire for the bloody chicken pluckin' contest.

No matter, by the time the girls stopped squealing dad was chopping the head off of the fifth and final chicken. It was a bloody frenetic flop fest!

The girls dashed into the screened back porch. Steve and Phil thought it would be cool to stand smack in the middle and try to dodge the blood.

Fred didn't want to get his jeans bloody. When the chicken bodies were all mostly still and lifeless, dad dipped them into a bucket of scalding water and tied them to a line.

"Come on, girls!" he beckoned "It's plucking time!"

What he should have said is "Come on girls! Get ready to pluck a chicken with one hand! You're going to need the other hand to hold your nose because the stink of the steaming pile of feathers could make an ogre cry!"

They were troopers. The surprising element in this account is that everyone stayed to pluck a chicken.

There were some near desertions at more than one point, but in the end, all five chickens got plucked by someone other than dad. He was damn proud of his creative genius.

Nobody remembers who won the contest. Everyone remembers the blood spewing corpses and the God-awful smell. When dad tried to arrange another chicken plucking contest, the girls decided they didn't need the money that bad.

# State Fair Escapade

## Sedalia, Missouri – 1972

It was our first full summer in Hicktown. Ma and Pa Upenleave decided that we all needed to do something fun in the summer of 72'. They also decided that mom would find a paying job, as soon as there were no children at home during the day. They planned on saving as much as possible each month in order to afford a better house. They probably would have looked for a more modern house, however, the rent they were paying to stay in the farmhouse was next to nothing.

One of the mandatory requirements for a fun getaway in the summer of 72' was – it had to be inexpensive. Dad's desire to spend a day at the Missouri State Fair came to fruition. There was one hitch. He couldn't afford to bring all eight of us. Mom would stay home and we would conduct a vote to decide who would go to the State Fair with dad. Everyone wrote the name of the person who they thought had been the most helpful around the house. The three with the most votes, were taking a trip!

The winners were Fred (13), Steve (10), and Denise (11). Phil expressed lament after the votes were tallied. Everyone else took it in stride.

The State Fair was everything the Upenleaves imagined it would be - and a heck of a lot more! They arrived Saturday at 11:00 AM., walked around for a while, just checking things out.

They wound up sitting in the bleachers at the race track. Dad was extremely interested in watching some horse and buggy races. Fred, Denise and Steve . . . not so much. The kids had their sights dead set on the carnival area. Dad gave them each $10.00 and words of wisdom. "Stick together and don't spend it all in one place." He and Fred synchronized watches and they were on their way.

The infinite possibilities for blowing the cash were mind numbing. So many games, rides, freaks and treats! Not all of the freaks were carnies, mind you. Their people watching stimuli was on the verge of overload. It was readily apparent why dad advised them to stick together.

As the three ex Air Force brats jaunted through the sprawling carnival, like first timers in a Las Vegas hotel, their discussions were on how they wanted to spend the cash. Denise's sweet tooth needed to be satisfied, Fred had a lust for a few perilous rides, and Steve was in the mood to win a stuffed animal playing those deceitful, no-skill necessary, carnie games. They were at odds about where to go first, when the smell of cotton candy put an abrupt end to the quarrel. Before they could say, "dang that smells like heaven," Denise was in line, holding her ten dollar bill and trying to calculate how much she would have left.

"Serpents from far-off lands, right before your very eyes!"

Fred and Steve rotated around to see who was doing the yelling. It was a short, round man who resembled the mayor of Munchkin land.
He was standing on a stage outside a tent with a banner advertising a snake charmer.

"See the snake charmer hypnotize a giant python! Witness the amazing feats that the deathly poisonous serpents will perform . . . within inches of the snake charmer! Come on in! The show starts in 10 minutes! Come one, come all!!"

It was like Fred and Steve were hypnotized. Denise watched them cross the strip to the snake charmer's tent without a word being said.

The two boys were standing among a group of about ten people who had gathered to listen, but there were no takers on the two dollar tickets. The barker needed to stoke the fire, so he pointed down at Steve and Fred. "You there, young man! Come on up here!"

Fred and Steve gave each other a worried look and pointed at each other. "Yes, yes! I'm talking to you, little freckle-faced boy."

Steve shook his head vehemently and muttered, "no thanks, I'll pass," just as Fred shoved him forward. What are big brothers for?

"Alright! Let's give the brave young man a hand!" The barker lead the crowd in a half-hearted round of applause, then helped Steve up on stage. "Have you ever held a poisonous snake, son?"

"No sir, but a Tarantula jumped on my leg once."

The crowd was amused, so was the Munchkin mayor. Steve's nervousness started to melt a little.

"Well, I can tell you're an adventurous lad." He reached into a box and came out with a narrow piece of rope.

The mayor then coiled it up and held it up for the crowd to see. "How would you like to see this rope turned into a serpent right before your very eyes!"

The crowd was warming up and Steve had to concur, that would be worth two dollars.
But to Steve's dismay, that Munchkin mayor stuffed the coiled-up rope down the front of Steve's shirt.

"What tha?" Is all Steve spit out. His nervousness spiked to a new level called desperation! Steve reached for the rope, but the mayor caught his hand.

"Who wants to see the snake charmer turn this rope into a slithering serpent now?" He solicited the crowd.

Steve was pretty much the only opponent to the scheme. Fred was a particularly vocal member of the growing crowd, cheering enthusiastically for the impossible. Steve was sweating bullets, keeping his eyes on the rope. The crowd was eating it up, so the mayor spun him around and sent him into the tent.

"Step right up and get your ticket to see the snake charmer! Show starts in three minutes!"

Someone on the inside untied the entrance flap and Steve stepped inside the tent.
It was just he and the snake charmer. He looked like Aladdin's Dad, but spoke perfect English. "You did good. Hand me the rope, and go out the back."

A wave of relief went through Steve, before he processed the information. "Wait, what?" Steve stammered as he handed him the rope. "You want me to leave?"

"Yes, of course. Hurry before they come in."
It didn't take him long to make a decision.

"I don't want to leave! Can I stay and watch the show?" Steve begged.

With a heavy sigh, Aladdin's father caved to his request.

"Ohhh, what the hell! Just stay in the background, ok?"

Steve smiled and watched the crowd file into the tent. Fred was among the suckers who paid to enter. Fred shuffled to Steve's side immediately. "Where's the rope?" he interrogated. "Did he already turn it into a snake?"

Steve knew what he wanted to say, but then he realized that everyone in the tent had their eyes glued to him, hanging on his response. Even the snake charmer!

"Ummm, yeah. I asked him to get it over with. He put the snake in that box over there!" Steve pointed to one of the black boxes that held the snakes. Aladdin's dad gave him a quick smile and a nod then started the show, as the last of the suckers came into the snake charmer's tent.

# Not Quite Venice

## Hicktown, Missouri – 1973

It was early spring, 1973. Life was grooving right along for us new-fangled country bumpkins. Of course there were a few things that we (especially the girls) were missing from our previous lifestyle like neighbors, convenience stores, a shower. The girls seemed to have gotten the proverbial short end, while most of the boys had become one with nature.

Fishing, hunting or exploring were leisure activities that could be undertaken within 100 yards of the farmhouse. There had been near record snow accumulation throughout the winter, then came the early spring rains. The Missouri river was already up into the tree lines and Hillers creek followed suit.

My family observed daily, with dread, the rising of the creek. Donna, Cindy and Denise knew the drill. They had moved so many times in their young lives it was second nature for them to gather their most precious belongings and store them in low-key carry-along containers. Their instincts proved correct because Hiller's Creek breached the multi-purpose event center. Now it was time for action! Most of the furniture was crammed into the two upstairs bedrooms. The rest was put on cinder blocks. The rabbit hutches had already been moved to the East side of the farmhouse.

Mom and dad found an old, rickety, abandoned house a few miles away to the North. Dad talked mom into squatting there to wait out the flood.

There was no running water in the abandoned house, which made our house seem like a posh hotel. The only difference between us and a homeless family was that we had a home to go back to.

That's right, PART THREE of The Homeless Upenleaves.

To the girls' dismay, we were only allowed to bring clothing and food. For them it was almost like having no reason to exist. Without the ability to clean up or apply makeup, the girls would try every angle known to mankind to ditch school. If any of their popular friends or cute guys saw them or, God forbid, got close enough to smell them, their lives would be shattered!
Might as well transfer to another school! Being homeless really sucked!

A couple of days went by and the water remained at the multi-purpose event field. Everyone cheered up when we were invited to eat dinner and bathe at a nearby neighbor's house. The girls were especially elated because it allowed them to shower some place other than school.

A few more days passed and the creek had not receded, but had not risen closer to the house either.

On the seventh day dad said, "the hell with it, we're going back!" The creek was still up in the multi-purpose field but everything was accessible. All the furniture was put back in place and life went on. The creek receded back to its normal level ... for a while. In this case, a while was two months before Hiller's Creek swelled beyond its banks again.

During our extremely unpleasant stay in the abandoned house we forged a friendship with the neighbors across the highway. The Smiths had been very cordial and giving to us. They had four kids, whose ages ranged from sixteen to five, so there were some connections among us kids as well. The Smiths were a hard-working catholic family too. They attended our church, in another small town to the East.

Mom invited them to join us for an Easter Sunday celebration. Egg hunt, dinner, pies and home-made ice cream for dessert. It would be mom's first chance in our new town to show off her cooking prowess.

When dad saw the creek breach its banks he called it off. "We need to start moving the furniture" he gravely advised.

"Over my dead body!" mom exclaimed. "I'm not moving until we're standing in that creek!" She was pretty confident that the creek would breach the field then taunt us for at least a week before receding. Don tried to reason with her, but mom's resolve was solid.

Bring it on! The Smiths brought a side dish and dessert. The egg hunt was nothing short of amusing as the smaller children were greatly distracted by the muddy water making its way closer and closer to the farmhouse. A few of the eggs got swallowed up by the water as easily as Marcia's delicious meal.

By the time the girls had the last dish put away, mom peered out the kitchen window and almost fainted. The creek was in our driveway.

You've never seen a more alarmed and frenzied bunch - especially since dad and the farmer who owned the land were already in the cellar turning off and sealing up the water heater.

Mr. Smith finally took charge by rallying the boys together to start carrying furniture upstairs, while the girls did their genuine best to impede the progress with their pacing, ranting and physical obstruction. It was a damn good thing the Smiths were there to help, as well as the farmer and his sons. What took a half-day two months ago was accomplished in an hour on this day. It's amazing what necessity can foster.

Everyone had to move their cars up the gravel road before the work was done, except for the farmer. His lifted 4x4 could go anywhere. Our stuff was off the ground floor, so we high-tailed it back over to the dry, old, rickety, abandoned house close to the Smiths to wait out the flood.

Wait we did. Hiller's Creek swept through the farmhouse and our garden, then meandered another 100 yards East to the middle of the farmer's soy bean field.

Dad and one of us kids would have to take a boat ride every other day for nearly three weeks to feed and water the rabbits. We had to use oars because there were so many shallow spots. Slopping around in knee-high mud and water was part of the deal too. Having to row through the shallow spots was the bummer, but getting muddy and seeing fish swimming in the house made the trip worthwhile.

Everyone except Donna and Chris took the farmhouse aquarium tour. The lucky ones got to spear fish with a pitchfork and, by the way, Don's rabbit hutch design (inspired by Donna's legs), kept the critters high and dry.

When the creek finally receded we were surprised to see the mud caked on the walls of our house was less than a foot high. That was the good news. Everything else . . . was bad news.

Together we scraped and scrubbed until the farmhouse was habitable and tolerated the musty smell for quite a while.

The flood of 73 did have some positive upshots: We worked together through the crisis resulting in stronger bonds and mutual respect; each person made daily sacrifices and we accepted what nature had dealt us.

The town had several community fish fries in the days after the flood. Up to fifty pound Carp and Buffalo fish were gigged out of the large pools of water left by the Missouri river.

Most importantly, dad and mom started planning to build their own house, beyond Hicktown . . . perhaps on a cliff.

Denise    Cindy    Donna

# Boring Campout

## Hicktown, Missouri - 1974

You know how campouts go. It sounds like a manly adventure full of fire-grilled goodies and ice cold beverages. Fred, Steve and Phil teamed up with their new buddy, Dan, for a Friday night campout. Fred (16) was the oldest. Dan was a year younger than Phil (12) and he lived in the heart of Hicktown.

There was a church, a grocery store, a town hall and a feed store for livestock in Hicktown. All within walking distance of Dan's house. So it was actually a town, not just a conglomeration of farmers. In fact, Dan's father wasn't a farmer.

The outdoor enthusiasts pitched a couple of tents, threw their sleeping bags inside and made a little camp fire. A little after dusk, Fred couldn't hold his bladder any longer so he stepped up on Dan's back porch and was about to walk into his house to take a leak.

"What are you doing, Fred?" Dan inquired.
"I gotta take a piss."
"This is a campout, man!" Dan reminded.
"Well, where should I go?"
"Walk out into the field." Phil suggested.

Everyone in Hicktown had a field and a propane tank next to their house.

Fred liked Phil's proposal and took him up on it. Actually, they all liked Phil's proposal.

Within seconds there was a piss fest. During the competition to see who could pee the furthest and for the longest amount of time, the subject of what to do next sparked an exchange of ideas. When the boys arrived back at the tent it was painfully obvious that they were bored, there was nothing to do in Hicktown at this hour, and Fred was the pissing champion.

"I've got an idea. Dan chimed in. Let's wait til midnight and take a walk through the old graveyard."
"Where is the old graveyard?" asked Fred.
"It's only about a mile up the road. Most of the people buried there were Negroes." Dan informed us.
"Sounds good!" Phil enlisted.
Fred glanced at his watch.
"Heck, it's only nine thirty. What are we gonna do for another two and a half hours?"

They played with the fire, told scary stories that everyone had already heard, talked about the girls that they liked and made fun of each other. 11:30 snuck up on them. At 11:45 they started walking up the gravel road. The anxiety of being in a turn of the century graveyard at midnight had been building since Dan suggested it. Now the boys were all hyper with anticipation and chock full of imaginative scenarios involving hungry, brain-eating zombies.

Finally the graveyard was in sight. By Fred's watch they had arrived a couple of minutes early, so they waited.

At precisely midnight they strolled silently to the rusted, broken down gates of the old graveyard like a band of looters slipping past a sleeping security guard. They were bunched together like Bonzo's bananas as one of the first tombstone became visible. It was a fairly large tombstone compared to the rest. Dan shined the flashlight on the stone to reveal the name. With generous sized font, the name etched in the stone was CROW. Perched on top of the tombstone was a live crow!

The reaction probably scared the ghosts of the old graveyard right back into their graves for decades, and the sound of them yelling and kicking up gravel as they ran the entire mile back to the tents undoubtedly woke up everyone whose house was along the way. They weren't stopping for anything. Once secure inside their respective sleeping bags, it was quite a while before they were sleepy at all. So they just laid there, reiterating what they saw and speculating about what it meant.

First thing after breakfast the boys paid a visit to that old graveyard. There was no sign of a hefty black bird then. Some of the folks buried there were born in the early 1800s. It was an interesting graveyard to visit . . . in the daylight.

Steve　　　Fred　　　Phil

That was one of the last episodes of Fred as an
innocent young man. For the next two years he
participated in several extra curricular activities
at high school. He was in R.O.T.C., which was a
readiness program for military officer candidates.
He was the boy's basketball manager, and he
worked at Mavrako's candy store in the city. Like
Donna, we didn't see much of him around the
farmhouse. He helped with the construction of our
new house on the weekends though.

# Country Life

## Hicktown, Missouri - 1975

Fresh air, fresh vegetables, homegrown meats, privacy, boundless, endless, adventures and country girls! Steve and Phil were in redneck heaven! One of the cutest girls in town, Jane, lived a quarter mile away, across the creek to the West. It was a mile by the gravel road. She had a pretty little sister, Judy, who was Teresa's age.

If Steve (14) or Phil (13) could have summoned the courage to ask Jane on a date or to join them on an adventure, the chances of her accepting the invitation were excellent, simply because, she was related to everyone else in town.

One dreary weekday evening in the spring of 1975, Steve finally got the cajones to do just that. He picked up the phone inside the farmhouse and guess who was chattering away on the party line? He waited until just the right moment . . . when Jane barked "Alright, who the hell's listening to us?"

"Oh, hey, it's Steve. Uhhhh, I was wondering if you might want to ride horses a little later?"

There was a moment of silence, then Jane countered. "Sounds good to me. I'll be over in thirty minutes."

"Great! I'll see you in thirty minutes."

"Now get the hell off the line!"

Steve slapped the phone down and darted outside to get his horse ready.

He was a handsome young stud. The mother was an American Saddle Pony, the father was an Appaloosa. He was a gingerbread brown color with patches of white on his legs and face. Steve named him Gingerbread. He was a little stubborn, like his mom and had an affinity for biting people. Other than that, he was a darn good horse.

Steve got him saddled up just before Jane arrived. When he spotted Jane walking her horse on the gravel road he mounted up and rode over to her. Jane turned her horse to the freshly plowed field and waved him on. "Come on! Let's go!" She dug her heels in and within seconds her horse was at a gallop.

"Heeyaaa!" Steve shouted as he dug his heels in and got Gingerbread to follow. Jane's horse was pretty fast but Gingerbread was holding his own. Steve knew that his horse wasn't use to running full bore on terrain this choppy, but so far so good!

He pulled up beside Jane, gave her a blissful smile then shot off the front of Gingerbread like a boy whose horse had just put on the brakes in a full gallop. The ground that his face mashed into was rough and unyielding, but he managed to get back on his feet walk over to Gingerbread and slug him right in the nose! Steve took Gingerbread's reigns, waved goodbye to Jane, and began the slow limp home.

As he made the painful trek, a past incident came rushing back to him as if it had just happened a few months ago.

Oh, wait . . . that's because it had just happened a few months ago. Our elder cousin, Jerry, who lived in Kansas and was somewhat of a cowboy, was visiting.

Steve was about to ride Gingerbread and Jerry, claiming that he wanted to be helpful, threw the saddle on and cinched it up. Steve got about fifty yards into the same field when Gingerbread finally exhaled. The worn saddle strap broke and Steve sailed off, flailing like a doomed trapeze walker. Cousin Jerry was on the ground as well, laughing his ass off.

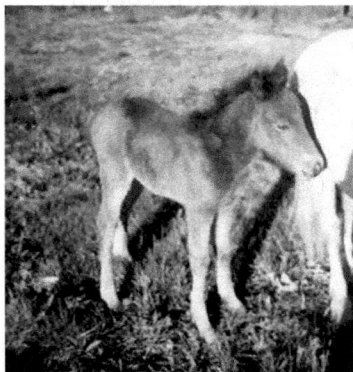

## Corn Cob Combat

In the barn, north of the pig pen, the boys would climb up into the hay loft and re-arrange the rectangle bails of straw to accommodate their recreational needs.

From Nerf basketball to corn cob fights, the land owner's tight rows of straw bails that hugged the aluminum roof were pulled down to be utilized in the erection of forts and tunnels which were critical components for any worthwhile corn cob fight. On any given day, the Upenleave males would summon their friends, scour the feeding trough area of the pig pen for corn cobs then climb the ladder to the hay loft.

Steve, Phil, Dan and Chris, who was only six, were going to have a corn cob free-for-all. Before they scattered to separate hideouts, Phil reminded them of Chris's age and vulnerability. He also laid down the law – no aiming for the head.
Everyone agreed to the terms then the three elders disappeared into separate corners of the loft, leaving Chris wondering, "ok what now?"

Suddenly, Dan popped up behind a stack of straw bails pointing to the opposite corner. "You get that corner over there, Chris. You better get moving before I nail ya," he played, with a corn cob pump fake. Chris did a duck and cover then he peeled out and leaped into his fortress.

Chris's fort was nothing but empty space behind a wall of straw bails, but there was a tunnel against the wall. He held his shirt in his teeth, dropped his corn cobs into the shirt hammock and began to shimmy on hands and knees through the tunnel. It made a left turn sending him toward the center of the barn, then it split. Chris was completely enthralled by the mazes and tunnels.

The tunnel he chose to follow next stopped in a small four foot square clearing. There were two more tunnels going in other directions but Chris decided to climb up a wall of straw and wait there. There were three bails in front of the wall to step on so he was at the top in no time.

His stay lasted about as long as Milli Vanillis' Grammy because Dan squirmed out of one of the other tunnels seconds later. Chris slid behind the wall undetected and took a few moments to summon his courage. When he was ready, he peeked over the top bail to assess the situation further. Granted, Chris had only just finished kindergarten.

Chris was the baby of the family and mom had certainly over-achieved in protecting him from the abuse of his siblings (Steve). He was quite the momma's boy despite having two very outgoing older brothers.

It was the moment of truth. He was ready to destroy his enemy so he eased into a standing position and caught Dan upright on the floor tucking corn cobs into his pants pockets. He aimed for Dan's midsection and rifled one at him.
Dan looked up just in time to get jolted! Right in the eye. Dan's shriek echoed all the way back to the farmhouse. Chris was frozen in a cringed position.

Steve and Phil arrived on the scene just in time to witness red-eye Dan's retaliatory strike.

That corncob came from down along the Gulf shores somewhere and struck Chris right in the rib cage. Chris immediately burst into tears while Dan cussed up a blue streak and groped at his eye. Phil and Steve tried their best to console their baby brother, and Dan expressed sincere regret for losing it . . . but, Chris's feelings were crushed and his ribs were aching so Phil escorted him home.

Dan and Steve waited just long enough to make sure Phil would have to explain the entire fiasco to Donna.

When mom returned home after her work day, Chris went right into his drunk floozy act, hiking up his shirt and showing off the red welt on his rib cage.

    "That is going to be a nice bruise, young man. How did that . . . never mind . . . STEVEN MARK!!! Come join us in the kitchen, right now!!"

Steve's ass was going to be grass regardless of the circumstances, so he shuffled in from the living room as mom was applying light pressure to the area around the welt for indications of a fracture.

Knowing Dan, he would have confronted my mother as soon as she got home, apologized for his actions and volunteered for kitchen duty. Unfortunately, Dan had left two hours prior.

    "Care to explain this? Your little brother was obviously struck by a hard object!" mother jabbed.

    "He has a mouth. Let him explain it," was Steve's detrimental counter.

Steam was piping out of mother's ears, so Chris decided to speak up. "Steve didn't do it. Dan did it."

Mom had a soft spot for Daniel, thus the steam subsided. Chris admitted that he asked to join the corn cob combat and the whole thing was an accident. Steve put the finishing touches on Chris's details by assuring mother that Dan's eye was much worse.
Steve still got grounded for allowing Chris to participate in the quickest corn cob fight in the history of Hicktown.


**Our School Bus**

Our bus ride to and from school was ludicrous. Approximately ninety minutes was wasted each morning and each afternoon if we had to ride the bus. The look on the other kids' faces the first time our platoon marched inside bus 41 was priceless! Seven nervous outsiders, most of us dressed in hand-me-downs or well-used attire (to put it nicely), shamelessly gawked at by the farmer's children in their new Levis and stylish shirts as we shuffled single-file through the aisle in pursuit of a seat.

By the time the bus rolled to a stop in front of our farmhouse in the afternoon, we were so anxious to have some privacy and utilize the space that rural living offered, we would fan out right off the bus and sometimes not see each other until dinner time. Just one of the perks of country life.

### Summer Funtasmic

School was out! Let the summer of 1975 commence! Kids got a full three month vacation back in those days.

Steve (14) and Phil (13) could hardly wait to hunt, fish, explore, get muddy, be rowdy and campout any night of the week, except Saturday because everyone had to go to church on Sunday at 8 A.M.

Donna (18) had graduated high school so she got an apartment in the city where she worked and attended the local university part-time.

Fred (17) was pretty much stuck at the farmhouse. With no driver's license or job to occupy his time and fatten his wallet, it was promising to be an extensively lackluster summer. Cindy and Denise echoed Fred's sentiment. The only difference was that Cindy was planning to stay with Cousin Jerry and his family in Kansas for a couple of weeks.

When dad would inquire about the events of the day at the dinner table, Cindy's voice was almost always the one that rose above and beat down the rest of us squabblers.

"Same old stuff, Dad. Watch T.V., lay in the sun, pull some weeds in the garden, try to keep Steve from harassing Chris." She complained.

"Yeah," Fred bolstered. "It sucks around here. There is absolutely nothing to do."

Dad rolled his eyes then gave Fred . . . 'the speech.'

This was the third summer in a row that Fred would leave himself open . . . actually, walk right into dad's speech.

"If I've told you once, I've told you a hundred times, boy. We are living smack dab in the middle of a bunch of farmers who will pay you to help them with their daily work."
"Show some initiative for Christ's sake! They will pick you up and bring you home! You will become stronger and wealthier! What part of that sounds bad to you, Fred?"
"All of it. I hate farm work."
Fred ate the rest of his dinner quickly and silently then excused himself.

That weekend, some of us went to visit dad's parents who lived about two hundred miles west of Hicktown. It wasn't planned, but dad came back with two extra kids. Dad's sister, Lois, had two boys and a girl. Her son Larry (13) was invited to join us for a funtasmic month at the farmhouse. Dad's other sister, Doris, had six children. Her son Daryl (13) expressed interest in exploring the surroundings of Hicktown as well. Steve and Phil were shooting the breeze with them about the finer points of killing a pigeon with one BB shot or how to do a 360 flip off the swing rope at Long Branch Creek. Before they knew what hit them, Larry and Daryl accepted the invitation with gusto. Lois and Doris seemed delighted to be alleviated of their precious teens for a month, so the cousins crammed themselves in the back of the station wagon and away they went.

Cousin Jerry and his wife, Sharon, gladly headed back to Kansas, with Cindy.

Back at the farmhouse, the routine continued for a few days. Steve, Phil, Daryl and Larry were romping around the countryside some days, sitting around watching T.V. on others.
Fred and Denise were so bored they would talk about the characters of the daily soap operas and their dramatic state of affairs as if they were part of the family. Dad finally got fed up with Fred's ambitionless plight and took matters into his own hands.

"Guess what you're doing tomorrow, boys?"

"I already know what I'm doing, Dad." Steve informed him. "Brooks and his Dad asked me to go fishing and camping with them, remember?"

"That's tomorrow?

"Yep. They're picking me up in the afternoon." "Well, that's a shame, son." Don grinned. "You are gonna miss out on the excitement at the Fulton State Hospital! That's right, boys," three of you are going to do some volunteer work at the hospital tomorrow."
"Each of you boys, that includes you, Steven, will have to go to work with me twice a week to work as a volunteer. I'll even let you choose which days you want to go. How do you like me now?"

Denise was desperately struggling with her urge to burst into a fit of hysteria while the boys struggled to process the idea of an entire day wasted at the looney bin for which, at the end of the day, they might receive a luke-warm "thank you."

111

Five pairs of evil eyes dead-panned on Fred, for they knew he was the reason dad was revoking their summer freedoms.

A torrent of arguments, complaints, what-ifs and how-abouts were volleyed back and forth between dad, mom and the boys. It was one of the longest dinner sessions of all time.
In the end, the prolonged deliberations were a stinking waste of time. They were going to be Fulton State Hospital volunteers!

A brief history of the Fulton State Hospital will augment the climax of this story, so here goes.

This information was obtained the Department of Mental Health at dmh.mo.gov/fulton/history.htm

In 1847, the Missouri General Assembly enacted legislation to establish an asylum for the insane in the center of Missouri. This institution would provide physical care for societal "lunatics." In 1851, Fulton State Hospital became the first public mental institution west of the Mississippi River. During the Civil War (1861) the hospital was forced to close. The building would be used to house soldiers.
A large number of individuals from the St. Louis area were returned home but the remaining "lunatics" had to be released back to their families or out on their own.

St. Louis built an asylum to house the large influx of these persons whose families could not care for them. Fulton just allowed these persons to filter back into society as best they could.

I'm not saying that the city of Fulton's forefathers are a bunch of lunatics, but . . . have you ever visited Fulton, Missouri?

The hospital reopened in 1863 and by 1880 "patients" worked and participated in recreational amusements on the hospital grounds.

These activities evolved into what we refer to as recreational and occupational therapy.

In 1934, some programs were kicked-off to educate the community about the prevention and treatment of mental diseases. One result of this community education was the development of a volunteer program. It allowed people to witness and identify with the disease of mental illness. Apparently the volunteer program was a tremendous success because volunteer interaction remains an important part of an individual's treatment today.

That's where the boys from Hicktown came in to the picture. Fred, Larry and Daryl piled into Don's pickup the next morning with visions of helping Don in the wood shop and mechanics garage, where he taught.

After being indoctrinated into the world of recreational therapy for societal lunatics, they learned that part of the time they would assist the physicians, instructors and caregivers with physical labor that somebody had to do.

The rest of the time they would interact with the patients doing some form of recreation.

Most of the time, they would be dancing with elderly ladies or playing checkers with the old men who wouldn't dance.

The first day was drawing to a close for the boys. It was an eye opening experience to say the least. For the final hour of the day, the three boys were escorted by a caregiver into a room full of geriatrics (elderly) patients and games; playing cards, checkers, puzzles, simple board games.

All the boys had to do was play some games with the old folks. Daryl was normally shy anyway, so it took all day for him to open up and start participating in the activities.

This was more his speed. He joined a man and a woman in a game of Chutes and Ladders. Larry challenged a friendly old geezer to a game of chess. Fred couldn't decide how he would participate, so he asked a nurse who was in the room with them.

"Why don't you just walk around and mingle with everyone." She advised. "One of them might invite you to play something."

"Alright, I can do that." Fred replied. There were approximately twenty patients in the room. Almost all of them were occupying themselves with one thing or another. Fred sauntered from person to person saying hello and sort of nervously initiating small talk. Surprisingly, they were too interested in the activities to chat much. Fred stopped next to a feeble, old, grey-haired man with scruffy grey stubble above his lip and on his chin. "Ahhh, you're doing a puzzle." Fred keenly identified.

The old man shot him a quick scowl, then resumed fumbling with the six piece puzzle called The Old Gray Mare. The nurse had helped him get the first two pieces in place.

When Fred approached she eased back and let the two males interact.

"Let's see. What's this puzzle supposed to look like?" Fred inquired.

As if he needed a picture to assemble a six piece puzzle.

He got no response from the old grey geezer, but instead of shoving off, Fred pulled up a chair and sat next to him.

The nurse gave him a supportive nod and moved on to intermingle with other patients. Fred just watched as the old man's frustration began to build with every failure to fit in the next piece.

To his credit, Fred lasted a good five minutes before intervening.

"Say, why don't you try that piece right there." Fred pointed to the obvious section that would fit.

The old gray geezer's head whipped around to face Fred, his eyes bulging with suppressed rage.

"Oh, go to hell, will Ya!" He shouted with a sense of meaning in his voice.

Fred shuffled backwards, still in his chair. He was mortified and embarrassed at the same time. The nurse and the caregiver were at the table instantly. Everyone in the room quit what they were doing to see what would happen next. Larry and Daryl smirked at each other, but contained their laughter. The nurse put her hand on the old man's shoulder.

"Well, Mr. Pimmerton. My goodness! Do you have anything else to say to this young man?"

Fred looked at her, wondering why she was provoking Mr. Pimmerton to continue cussing him out. Mr. Pimmerton, who was shaky and flustered, just pointed at Fred and mumbled incoherently. Finally, the caregiver motioned for Fred to follow him away from the scene of the crime. Fred was more than willing to escape the celebrity spotlight. Daryl and Larry joined Fred and the caregiver in a small circle.

"What was that all about?" Daryl pressed.
    "All I did was try to help him with that stupid puzzle," frazzled Fred explained.
    "Listen, Fred. I'm sorry that Mr. Pimmerton was rude to you," the caregiver appeased.
"The reality is that the old man hasn't spoken a word for more than two years. We've put him through every one of our therapy classes. Man! You really got under his skin in a hurry. I'm sure the nurse will agree with me that you should try to interact with him again soon."

Fred couldn't believe his ears, while Daryl and Larry had to leave the room to release their uproars.
    "I don't feel like I wanna be here anymore." Fred shared with disheartened emotion.
    "Yes, well, your first day has had a few trials. Why don't you go relax in the break-room. Your day is over pretty soon anyway. You can get a fresh start tomorrow."

"Ok, but I meant that I don't want to come back here at all."
With a raised eyebrow, the caregiver retorted, "we'll see what your father has to say about that."

Fred shuffled away to the break room murmuring about what dad would say.
The ride home was exceedingly amusing for dad. All three boys had a humorous episode to share about one of the other boys.
Daryl finally got the nerve to approach an old woman in a wheel chair by himself. "Hello, maam. "Are you having a good day?" He asked, forcing an awkward smile.
"Is that you, William?" She grinned with outstretched arms.
"Oh, thank you lord! I've been praying that you would come to visit! Come come, give your mother a hug!"
Daryl glanced over his shoulders knowing full well that the old woman thought he was her son. He looked directly into her elated eyes . . . and had no idea what the hell to do.
He couldn't decide whether to play along with the outlandish lie and make her day, or tell her the truth, thus bursting her euphoric bubble and ruining her day. So he stood there. Right there within inches of her groping fingers, his eyes bounced around in their sockets, rummaging for a suitable response. "Uhhhhh", was all that he could muster.
A few more seconds passed before one of the nurses rescued Daryl with a proper introduction to Mrs. Casselberry. Daryl breathed a sigh of relief. Mrs. Casselberry wheeled herself away from Daryl with a loud, disgruntled HARUMPH!

Larry invited a middle-aged brunette with flowing hair to dance a slow one, the surprise came when a middle-aged man turned around and accepted Larry's offer.
I doubt that Larry has ever been a darker shade of red. Of course, Fred's 'Little Gray Mare' incident kept them laughing the entire drive home.

That summer would prove to be anything but lackluster. Volunteering at the Fulton state Hospital gave the boys an entirely different perspective on life and the inhabitants of their planet.

## Tanning in the Field

It was a mild summer day in the country. Denise decided it was perfect weather for browning her skin. On this particular day, Denise would go for the gusto and sunbathe topless.

Having four brothers who did not have lives would make the task more difficult than just plopping down in the back yard. She would need a spot far enough away from the house that one of her brothers would not see her from the yard and bombard her with something from the hog-slop bucket. It also had to be far enough away from the gravel road to avoid the wandering eyes of a neighbor driving by. She explored the regions behind the house to North, since the gravel road ran east and west and was on the south side of the house.

The North side of the chicken coop would have concealed her nicely, but she couldn't handle the stench.

Wandering a little further North she spotted a clearing next to the soy bean field. This spot was perfect.
She could only see the top of the house because the farmer who owned the land had a garage between her and the house.

Denise got her towel situated, sat down and scanned 360 degrees. All clear. She unfastened her bikini top oiled herself and stretched out under the midday sun.

She must have fallen asleep, because when she opened her eyes she felt somewhat groggy. She smiled at the thought of having found the perfect spot!

Her eyes almost closed again when some movement alerted her. She turned her head toward the farmer's garage and her eyes jolted open.
The farmer who owned the land was admiring the view from a few yards away.

"Oh, hello, Denise." He greeted her casually while her jaw dropped. Then he turned, got into his truck and drove away.

From that day forward the farmer always had a warmer smile for Denise. Go figure.

## Good Little Thief

Steve, Phil and Chris were looking pretty shaggy, and being an ex-military man, dad liked to see his sons with short, tight haircuts. The previous summer (1974) he had purchased a barber's kit. Dad would rather work a little harder to save a few pennies. He was old-school and damn proud of it. The first lawnmower he purchased was an ancient all-mechanical, two-wheel, push mower. He bought it at a farm auction for five dollars.

As I was saying, the previous summer he had solicited the boys to volunteer to receive the first Don Upenleave haircut.
There was a sudden sense of urgency among the boys to accomplish procrastinated chores. Someone placed one of Teresa's favorite dolls in the haircut chair, on the backyard sidewalk. Dad didn't take the hint and Teresa didn't see the humor. When the dust settled, Steve, Phil and Chris looked like Marines on the first day of boot camp.

The cutest girl in town delivering 100 free packages of Topps baseball cards wouldn't have made the boys smile.

Eventually dad honed his skills with an electric trimmer. He also became more sensitive to their attitudes about military-style haircuts.

In the summer of 1975, Steve and Phil talked dad into taking them to the barber shop in Mokane.

Phil and Steve got in the barbers' chairs first.

The barbers followed dad's instructions to the letter. While Steve and Phil weren't ecstatic about their looks, it was a definite improvement over last summer's hair cut.

"Can we go to the store, Dad?" Phil pleaded.

"Ohhh, I don't see any harm there. Just the store. Don't go wandering around, you here?"

"We won't. We'll come right back."

Dad and little Chris hopped into the barber chairs while Steve and Phil trolloped out the door.

They each had some loose change and had their minds set on purchasing a package of baseball cards with bubble gum for a dime.

Once inside the small store, they were in no hurry to get to the baseball cards, which were on a rack right in front of the checkout counter. They browsed the candy aisle, fantasized about making themselves a big frothy soda at the soda fountain then stood doe-eyed in front of the magazine rack forcing a couple of other boys to move along.

After a couple of minutes the shop owner barked at them. "If you ain't got the money to buy one, move along, youngsters!"

The bubble gum was in their mouths even before they got out of the store. As they walked along the street, they were so focused on the baseball cards that they failed to notice the two boys that had followed them out of the store.

"Hey! Who did ya git?" Came a voice from behind them.

Steve and Phil swiveled around to amiably confront the stalkers. It was the infamous Laudermill brothers, Gary and Pat.

Gary was Steve's age, but damn near a foot taller. Pat was two years younger and tough as rawhide. They were disheveled, street punks, whose parents had no business being parents.

"Let me see who you got?" Gary requested with an outstretched hand.
Phil and Steve glanced at each other. It was obvious that they didn't trust Gary Laudermill with a pile of horse manure, so they sure as hell weren't gonna hand him their newly acquired baseball cards.

"Ahhhh I didn't really get anybody good. Mike Schmidt is the best one in here." Steve enlightened him.
"We're just gonna go back to the barber shop." Phil added. They spun around and started walking.
"Hold on a minute!" Gary protested. "I was just about to ask you two fellers a important question."
Gary and Pat scooted around them, stepping in front and halting their progress.
"You see, my little brother hasn't eaten anything today and we ain't got no food at home being that our pa spent the rest of his paycheck on the whiskey. You boys got any change left to help us out?"

Phil and Steve glanced at each other again. Steve felt the two coins in his right pocket . . . 15 cents, enough for an ice cold bottle of Nehi Orange soda back at the Hicktown general store.
"Sorry man, we spent it all," Steve lied.

"That's weird. Coulda' swore old man Burns gave you some change back from the cards. You wouldn't lie to me would ya?" Gary pressed.

"We need to get back to the barber shop!" Phil exclaimed, while trying to step around Pat. Pat moved with him and held out his arm to corral Phil. Steve and Gary did the same dance, causing Gary to lose his patience. Gary pushed Steve back and doubled up his fists.

"You don't wanna test me, shit stain! I'll be your worst nightmare!" Gary threatened.

Steve had his fingers on the 15 cents and was easing his hand from his pocket when dad bounded down the concrete steps from the barber shop with shaving cream smeared on only half of his face. He snatched Gary up like an eagle snaring a field mouse. Pat took off like a chicken in a crocodile pit. Dad flipped the young street thug around, bent him over his shoulder and hauled him into the barber shop.

The bald barber chuckled. The barber with bags under his eyes just shook his head in disgust.

"What do you have there, Don?" The bald barber jested.

"I believe I have me a little tough guy."

"I believe you have the dirtiest little thief in town," the baggy-eyed barber chimed in.

"So you're a bully AND a thief, huh young man?" Dad queried.

"Let me go, mister! You'll be sorry ya ever messed with me!"

"Oh I'm already sorry, cuz your stench is so strong my eyes are watering. When was the last time you had a bath, boy?"

"Screw you, old man!" Gary gnashed.

At that, dad grabbed his ankle, dangled him upside down and got a grip on the other ankle. Some coins clattered on the tile and after a couple of vigorous shakes a pocket knife, then a Playboy magazine hit the floor.

Chris was laughing hysterically in his barber's seat, and the barbers were thoroughly amused as well.
Phil was real proud of his old man, Steve snatched up that Playboy magazine before the two second rule expired.

The moment dad set Gary back on the floor he scraped up his belongings and flew out the door. Phil had to dodge laterally to get out of his way.

During the drive home, Phil was explaining the details of the confrontation to dad. When he was finished dad asked, "what was that magazine you picked up, Steven?"

Phil and Steve shot each other a knowing glance before Steve replied, "what magazine?"

After a pause, dad shook his head. "I'm probably better off not knowing anyway."

Sly smiles crept onto their faces. Later they would privately thank Gary, the good little thief, for providing them with their first exposure to gorgeous naked women!

# Don't I Know You?

## Madison, Wisconsin - 1976

The friends that Donna made back when she was thirteen in Sun Prairie, Wisconsin liked to get together at one of the girl's houses whose parents were, what's the word? **absent**, most of the time. Teen boys and girls alike would converge on the house as soon as the parents drove away.

At first they were into board games and video games, like Atari. That evolved into Ouija board séances. Soon enough the older boys who frequented the joint got bored with the lame tortured spirits and talked some of the girls into playing strip poker. Donna had played cards with Grandpa in Monona a couple of times. She could beat those boys at their own game. Easier said than done! It was pretty risqué for a thirteen year old to be playing strip poker, but Donna insists that she never parted with her bra or panties.

At this point in her life, Donna was a high school graduate working two minimum wage jobs and going to a local university part-time. With little money to spare on a decent summer getaway, she decided to visit our family up in Wisconsin. She made plans to stay with mom's younger sister, aunt Jeanine.

She and Jeanine were at a mall in Madison, Wisconsin, close to Jeanine's apartment. Donna and Jeanine walked into one the shoe stores.

Donna was trying on a pair of pumps when one of the salesmen approached the ladies. "Can I be of assistance?" he gestured.

"No thanks. We'll let you know if we need something," Jeanine replied.

"Don't I know you?" the young man continued.

Donna looked him over then looked back at Jeanine. "I don't even live here. I'm visiting my aunt."

"Your name is Donna, isn't it?"
Donna was impressed.

"How did you know that?"

"You're Donna Upenleave. I would recognize you anywhere!" By the way, you sure lived up to your name."
Both Jeanine and Donna were flabbergasted.

"You don't recognize me? I'm Dale Stroud. We use to play strip poker at Angie Mason's house! In Sun Prairie."

Donna looked up at Jeanine with an embarrassing grin. Jeanine shook her head.

"How  . . . old were you?" Jeanine pried.

"Oh, I was probably fourteen or fifteen," Dale interjected.

"I was talking to my niece, if you don't mind."

"Oh," Donna stalled nervously. I was thirteen. But it wasn't strip, strip poker. It was more like . . ."
Donna was at a loss for words and Dale was trying to bail her out by wishy-washily shaking his head then nodding in agreement.

126

"I think we're leaving now." Jeanine informed them.

"Yeah, we should probably, uhh." Donna stammered.

"Well, it was great to see you again!" Dale shouted, as Jeanine dragged Donna from the shoe store.

Jeanine managed to pry the details from Donna about the teen parties at Angie Mason's house, after which, she was cool enough to keep the particulars to herself.

# Helmendok

## Hicktown, Missouri - 1976

It was dusk when Phil (14) and Steve (15) spotted the old house from the well-worn path next to the vast field of soy beans. They were just exploring the territory approximately five miles from their house and this was an exhilarating adventure, so they parked the motorcycle in the brush and started the ascent.

As it came into view, their tensions heightened. The house looked like it belonged in Amityville. Perched atop a weed infested hill and looming over miles of farmland to the North and the mighty Missouri River to the South.

The climb was about 100 yards of undisturbed, waist-high weeds, but there was no hesitation between the boys. They had explored their share of abandoned houses, but there was a mystique about this one, a sense of something extraordinary awaiting them.

They were half-way up when Phil stopped dead in his tracks, his hand shot up with a rigid pointing finger. "Whoa! Check it out!"
"What?"
"Upstairs."
Steve saw the faint image of a man with an Army green ball cap moving back out of view from the upstairs balcony door which had a glass insert in the upper half.
"What did you see?" Steve wanted to know.

128

"There was a man in an Army jacket and cap looking down on us." Phil shot back.

"Well, you want to keep moving or . . . what? It's gonna be dark soon."

"Let's check this place out real quick. We can come back in the daytime."
Steve agreed and they hastened the pace to the top. When they finally stepped up on the front porch there was a mutual acknowledgement of the feat in getting there.

Taking heavy breaths, they eased over to peak through the large picture window to the front room. The first thing they saw was a couch. Over the cushions a crumpled, stained sheet was spread . . . and there was a knife! A large kitchen knife that appeared to be thrust into the heart of a person under the sheet whose blood was now a sickly brown color.

Steve was the first to do a 180 degree pivot and leap in the same motion. The words spewing from his innocent mouth sounded like a long-haul sailor in a Bangkok watering hole.

Philip was right on his tail but Steve didn't know it because he wasn't looking back. They were in full sprint mode, taking cheetah strides, when

Steve heard a commotion behind him that sounded like a whole patch of weeds being violently disturbed.

Sure enough, Phil had bitten the dust. His recovery was so fast you would have thought the man in the army cap was chasing them with the murder weapon.

Seconds later, they were bent over beside the motorcycle, panting and speculating in their minds what it was that they just witnessed.

 Phil felt the blood trickle into his eye, wiped his brow and grimaced at his bloody fingers.

"Pretty nasty cut, man." Steve informed. "Let's get outta here!"

On the way home they decided to keep the gruesome discovery a secret until they had a chance to come back and verify what they were 98 percent sure of.

Keeping their lips sealed wasn't easy among eight family members, but they pulled it off and conjured up the courage to go back the following day.

The Helmendok house, the name given by the locals after the last family who inhabited it, was much less daunting in broad daylight. It also turned out to be much more vacant.

There were no signs of a person who had been stabbed through the heart, or a blood-stained sheet, or even a drop of blood. Phil didn't know whether to feel relieved, cheated or confused.

There was a mixture of those feeling permeating his thoughts as the boys shuffled from room to room, finding a lot of useless debris, some beer cans and drinking cups and some old clothes in one of the upstairs rooms.

Steve's thoughts were guarded because he was privately smug in the knowledge that the hoax he and Dan had concocted worked to perfection.

He felt guilty about the cut over Phil's left eye but at least it didn't require stitches. He would keep the cruel truth from his younger brother for the better part of a week, time enough to pull the hoax on Brooks, a friend who lived just a couple of miles away from Helmendok.
He too, fled like a rat from a sinking ship, but wasn't quite as worried about the ramifications compared to Phil.

Dan spilled the beans to Brooks later that day and Steve finally confessed to Phil the following day. It was no doubt, one of Steve's crowning achievements in his chronicle of gags, jokes and hoaxes . . . and the payback would be forthcoming.

# Well I'm, Well I'm, Shorry Ma'am

## Fort Leonard Wood, Missouri – 1976

Grandma Rachael and Aunt Jeanine were visiting us in Hicktown, but mom wanted to do something special, away from the farmhouse. She and dad rented a cabin for a weekend at Fort Leonard Wood, an army base close to the Lake of the Ozarks.

At this point in our family history, Fred had just graduated from high school and was in Marine Corp boot camp. Cindy (17) did not make the trip because she had an honest-to-goodness date Saturday night with a boy she had recently met.

Cindy and Denise spent a good percentage of their adolescence competing for things. This love/hate relationship was heavily incited by the stark disparity of their physical beings.

Cindy was skin and bones with fine, straight, lifeless hair. She wore glasses that resembled the ones Adrian wore in the movie ROCKY. Her personality had improved in her teen years. She was sociable and friendly. We had all developed various defense mechanisms to ward off adverse emotions; rejection, loneliness, worthlessness. It was a product of our nomadic lifestyles. Sometimes, the kids we thought were our friends, didn't even say goodbye to us. Other times, we didn't bother making friends, because we didn't want to feel hurt again.

Some of us kids were pretty stealth with our defense mechanisms. Not Cindy. She wore her emotions on her shirt sleeve.

She was still as stubborn as ever and habitually voiced her opinion about . . . well, everything. One of her most frequent complaints was that we lived so far out in the sticks, no boys would drive that far to pick her up for a date. That was usually the cue for dad to remember something he had misplaced and for mom to ask Cindy to help her with something. Of course that was Cindy's cue to go upstairs and finish her homework. Such a vicious cycle.

Denise was on the other end of the spectrum. Her body had filled out nicely. She was trim and pretty with curly, blondish-brown hair. Her demeanor was adventurous and flirtatious.

Denise (16) was the oldest child on this outdoorsy excursion. Within the first few hours of us settling in to our cabin by the lake on Friday afternoon, Denise had, of course, met a boy. It was becoming apparent to the rest of us that Donna had trained her well.

It was Saturday afternoon. Dad, Steve, Phil and Christopher were trying their luck with fishing poles. Mom needed some groceries, so she and the rest of the females hopped into our blue station wagon and headed down the gravel road to the market.

About half way there, an Army jeep was rounding a sharp corner too aggressively and mom was in the wrong place - going around the same corner. The driver of the jeep tried to get over, but the gravel was unforgiving. He slammed into the side of our station wagon and bent the left front wheel. The driver's door wouldn't open and the car was immobile. Thankfully, nobody was hurt.

The driver of the jeep was an Army sergeant (E-5). His name was Jimmy Stewart. He was sweating bullets, apologizing, and checking to make sure everybody was alright. He swore it wasn't normal, but he was stuttering, just like the actor.

Mom knew there would be punishment handed down to Jimmy Stewart, because it was clearly his fault. He knew it as well. All the ladies felt sorry for him, but that didn't change anything. Jimmy Stewart contacted an Army dispatcher, and a team of investigators came to the scene then gave the ladies a ride back to the cabin.

The car would have to be towed to a garage for repairs, so dad and mom would have to rely on Donna or Cindy to bring everyone home. Cell phones weren't invented yet, and we didn't have an answering machine, but as luck would have it, Cindy answered the phone at the farmhouse. Man was she sorry she did. When Cindy hung up the phone, she was highly agitated! She was going to have to cancel her date, drive down to Fort Leonard Wood, and drive back with her car stuffed to the brim with everybody and everything! "AAAHHHHH!!!!"

The lake crew could have stayed until Sunday, but the adults opted to get home as soon as possible.

When Cindy arrived at the cabin Saturday evening, she was calm and somber.

That was before Denise threw a hissy-fit. Tears streamed down Denise's cheeks as she pleaded with Mom to stay another day. Everyone knew Denise's motive for wanting to stay – the boy. It didn't bother the guys, they were pretty sure mom and dad would just tell her to suck it up and get in the car, but Cindy took Denise's actions a trifle more seriously.

So seriously, that Jeanine had to restrain her to keep from knocking Denise's block off!
I can't believe her!" Cindy yelled, trying to free herself. "Little Miss, Married at Five, is upset because she can't spend one more day with another boy that she just met?" Meanwhile I had to cancel a date tonight that was . . . let's see . . . my first real date since we moved to this miserable town! Let me go, so I can shove those tears up her . . ."
"Calm down, girls!" Mother insisted, with a somber look herself. This situation is out of our hands. We are lucky that nobody was hurt in that accident, so let's thank the Lord and keep it that way."

We kept Denise away from Cindy for the remainder of the trip. As for the station wagon, the Army paid for the tow and the repairs, but the transmission never quite worked the same afterwards. Dad suspected that the towing company was at fault.

The issue was never resolved, so we drove the station wagon for another year or so before trading it in.

## Sneaky Plan

### Hicktown, Missouri – 1976

In the fall of 76', during the school year, Denise managed to talk, cajole and bribe mom and dad into letting her use one of the two family cars to go on a date with a boy in the city. The details regarding why the boy could not venture so far out in the sticks to pick her up are irrelevant. Denise was given a midnight curfew and several threats of bodily harm and hard labor if she AND THE CAR were not home by the bewitching hour!

Denise was elated that she had won her parents trust and was headed down the gravel road at 7 P.M.

It was well before midnight when mom and dad heard the sound of a car pulling in and parking next to the house. Mother rolled over in bed and rubbed dad's arm. "I think our girl is home". She smiled. Dad opened one eye and peeked at the clock. 11:40.

"Amazing", he murmured, then allowed himself to drift away again.

No telling how much time had passed when dad felt the massive shifting of the tectonic plates beneath the earth's . . . oh, that was just mom shaking him.

"Wake up, Don! Come on, wake up!"

"What is it, woman?" he sputtered in his agitated voice.

"We heard Denise pull in 30 minutes ago, and the car is in the driveway . . . but she isn't in her bed. Where could she be?

Dad sat up and rubbed his face. "For cryin' out loud! How should I know?"

Mother pulled some clothes out of the closet and set them on the bed for dad.

There was an old wooden bridge over Hiller's creek 200 yards south of the farmhouse along the gravel road. It was a familiar spot for our adventures.

At the moment, there was a VW Beetle parked next to it, the windows clouded with steam. Inside, Denise was buttoning her blouse while sliding from the back seat to the front passenger seat.

"Gotta get home now, Tim," she sighed. "Yeah, ok, damn! It's 1:45." Tim chuckled.

"Thanks for . . . everything." Denise cooed. "That party was so cool! I think I'm still stoned."

"Hell I know I am. Richard gets the most badass weed! He won't tell me where he gets it either, the prick!"

"Hey, at least he turned us on, man," she mused.

Tim's VW crept around the final turn before the farmhouse then eased to a stop in-line with the front porch. Denise closed her door ever-so-quietly and tip toed across the gravel road to the front yard. Tim mimicked her.

They were right in front of the porch when Tim put his arm on Denise's shoulder and leaned in for a good-night kiss.

The porch door opened. Dad stepped out, holding a shotgun and wearing an angry scowl. Tim's arm flew off of her shoulder like a Scud missile.

"I hope you have some religion, boy, cuz you need to start saying your prayers." Don assured him, while bringing the rifle barrel up. "What have you been doing with my daughter?"

Tim backed up with his palms facing forward. "I uhh, we uhhhh." Tim panicked and bolted for his car. Dad squinted at Denise, then gave chase.

"NOOOO! Dad!!!" Denise wailed.

Tim went around the back of the VW, pulled his door open and almost made the lunge, but dad still had a little spring in his step.

Moving around the front of the car, dad thumped the door with the butt of the shotgun, slamming it shut!

"Stay still, boy! Now I'm gonna shove this shotgun barrel right up your keester!"

"Come on, Dad", Denise begged pathetically, "leave Tim alone, please?"

Dad made his move. Tim wasn't about to leave his precious Beetle with this irate, destructive old man flailing away, so he just circled around it with dad on his heels. Tim was young and quick so dad tried to stop and double back on him but Tim was suddenly alert and thus reversed his field. Around and around they went, like a bad cartoon.

Denise was so embarrassed she didn't know whether to cry or faint, so she crumpled to the ground, sat cross legged and buried her face in her hands.

Finally, dad got winded and stopped at the hood to catch his breath. Tim seized the opportunity, dove into the driver's seat and shoved the stick into gear. Dad gave the VW's hood a couple of shotgun dents before Tim managed to fantail out of there, kicking up dust all the way to the highway.

Denise's sneaky plan really backfired. She got grounded, of course. Then when she finally was able to talk to Tim, he kicked her to the curb.

Although she thought it was the end of the world, it was just a minor setback. That was her last sneak attempt.

# Get Some Tires!

## Hicktown, Missouri - 1981

Steve and Phil were working class dogs out of high school. Both were peons in their respective fields but worked the day shift. Since Phil didn't have a car yet, he hitched a ride with Steve.

It was a wintry day around 4:00 P.M. They were trying to get home in the midst of a snow storm. Traffic was heavy on that two lane highway to Hicktown. Steve's recently purchased 1975 Chrysler Cordoba needed tires, but Steve procrastinated because he had other priorities; a new coat, a few new cassettes, a little weed and plenty of beer for the weekends.

Phil was asleep in the passenger seat while Steve had all he could handle trying to keep his sled on the road. His bald tires made it seem like they were ice skating perilously close the oncoming traffic and his windshield smearers were driving him crazy.
Suddenly the front end skated toward the side of the road and just kept going. Steve was helpless at the wheel. She slid until the tires found some traction, then the beast lurched forward straight down the fifteen foot embankment.

Phil might have slept through the entire ordeal had Steve had not taken that opportunity to scream into his ear "Holy Shit, man!! We're screwed!!"

That brought Phil to life. He was quick to realize the jeopardy that his life was in at the moment.

"WHAT ARE YOU DOING?" he demanded.
"Yeahh, I got tired of driving in that monotonous line of cars up there."
Phil looked back at the monotonous line of cars up there. "WHAT?"
"We slid off the road, jackass! Better put your seat belt on for once."

Steve ran his options through his mind . . . then he punched the accelerator to get the beast up to maximum speed in a ditch, in six inches of snow. They were building momentum and starting to calm down when Phil spotted a culvert in their path about 40 yards ahead. Steve waited as long as he could, just missing the culvert as they started the ascent. So far, so good, they were gaining confidence and wearing nervous grins at the half way point. Vehicles on the highway were slowing down to allow them access.

"I bet they're getting a good laugh out of this" Phil jeered.
"We're gonna be the ones laughing when we pull into our driveway."
The beast was slowing to a crawl but the front tires were on the highway! Steve had no choice but to keep the pedal to the metal as the traffic behind them eased back to let them in. The left rear tire was on the road and the right rear tire was . . . spinning in the snow.

"NO! NO! NO!" They shouted in unison as they pounded the steering wheel and the dash board.

They were stuck and even more humiliated than before.

A few cars went by them when the oncoming traffic cleared, but a farmer in a 4X4 pickup stopped in front threw a chain under the chassis and pulled them onto the highway. Phil shook his hand, then slugged Steve.

Steve managed to keep her on the road the rest of the way, and with his next paycheck, he sprung for a set of all weather radial tires.

# The Four Compadres

## Mokane, Missouri – 1981

Mokane is a small country town a short distance from Hicktown. Every summer on a designated weekend, a large carnival would come to town and set up just north of the main highway. They had a vast empty field with which to operate so the rides and games could be spread out nicely. The road into Mokane was a narrow two-laner with ditches on each side. The ditches were fifteen to twenty feet deep coming off of the highway. The closer you got to downtown the more shallow the ditches became until they leveled off completely. The downtown area was a good 200 yards north of the highway. The carnival was set up on the east side of the two-laner between the downtown and the highway.

It was a Friday night, but not just any Friday night. It was the world's fair night that the boys from Hicktown had been looking forward to for weeks. Steve (19), Phil (18) Dan (17) and Brooks (16) would win some stuffed animals then cruise around looking for a pack of pretty girls to impress with their generosity. The plan was to get them on the Ferris wheel, steal some kisses and see where it went from there. They were all handsome kids and they had tasted success in the past!

The 75' Cordoba with brand new tires and a decent stereo was a real pimp daddy cruiser, until Steve let some crazy chick talk him into letting her drive.

She veered right into a car that was passing them and that was the end of the pimp daddy cruiser.

But for now, Steve pulled off the main highway on the road to Mokane and made an immediate right turn into the parking area. It was almost dark when they popped the trunk and each retrieved a cold one from the cooler.

"I don't want to go in just yet," said Steve.

"Let's listen to some tunes," Dan advocated. Dan had talked Steve into buying the Devo cassette and Steve had most of the popular rock cassettes as well.

The Hicktown boys were feeling a little more than just a beer buzz at the moment. They had planned and executed taking something with a little more of an edge than alcohol. It was a small dose, but for Steve and Phil, it was the first time ever. Their buzz was so intense they stayed in the car and rocked out until well after dark, playing the rolls of Devo, Aerosmith and Van Halen. After an hour of jamming, they finally talked each other into exploring the Mokane World's Fair.

They were standing in the gravel discussing the strategy when a car flying down the highway whipped onto the road to Mokane, swerving and squealing its tires.

Their undivided attention shifted to the street where an unruly driver who barely managed to stay out of the ditch coming off the highway, proceeded with undue acceleration down the narrow two-laner with cars parked on each side of it.

The buzzed crew looked at each other with <u>Final Destination</u> grimness, then witnessed the wild-ass fool scrape a car on the left, overcorrect and pinball off of a car on the right, sending it into the ten foot ditch, then slam into another car back on the left, sending it into the ditch as well. Apparently the accelerator was stuck, because during the second parked car's roll to the bottom of the ditch, the offending vehicle launched over the top of it and landed upside down.

With an extended jaw Phil shook his head. "Sure, that just happened."

The Hicktown boys were already in full sprint as the wreckage settled. Since the accident occurred right next to the parking lot, they were, without a doubt, the closest bystanders and possibly the only witnesses.

When Phil caught up, they weren't worried about the cars that were static, just the offending vehicle. As soon as they reached the bottom of the ditch gasoline fumes choked their deep breaths down to shallow ones.
"This isn't real," Steve refused to believe.

He closed his eyes and tried to relax as the sound of an engine trying to turn over eased his pulsating adrenaline. There it was again, the sound of someone trying to start . . .

"Shit!" Brooks screamed. He's trying to start his car!"

They made a mad dash for the driver's side of the overturned vehicle.
It was dark, but they could see that it was a woman, she was bleeding from a wound on her head and she was trying to start her inverted and crumpled hell wagon.
The driver's door suffered irreparable damage and couldn't be opened, so Brooks and Dan slid their fingers under the slightly open window and pulled on it until it shattered.

At that instant a handful of men and boys from the carnival grounds who had heard the tumultuous disturbance descended into the ditch cursing and clamoring. "Hey, what the hell's going on over there?" One of the men demanded. He pulled out his Bic lighter and sparked a flame to look inside the cars.
Steve freaked, rushed over to him and knocked the lighter out of his hand.

"Are you trying to kill us, man? You smell the fumes, right?"

"Uhhh, sorry, man," was his sorry response.

After attempting to converse with the disoriented driver, Dan and Brooks made the simple assessment that she wasn't crazy after all . . . she was wasted! Drunk beyond stupidity!

They reached in, grabbed whatever they could grasp and pulled her out kicking and screaming. She was way too drunk to put up much of a fight, so they dragged her a good distance away from the vehicle, plopped her ass in the grass and held her arms.

Phil was high enough . . . I mean . . . brave enough to go back to the hell wagon to remove the keys from the ignition. That brought about a sigh of relief from the crowd of folks hovering around the two Hicktown boys and the drunken hellcat.

"All the cars are empty!" One of the strangers reported. "Is that dude drunk?"

"That's a World's Fair understatement." Brooks retorted. "And the dude is a chick!"

The stranger stomped forward. "All I know is somebody's gonna pay for the damage to my Trans Am that's laying in the ditch over there! And that somebody is . . . Hey, I know this bitch! She's my cousin!"

A distant siren getting closer by the second interrupted him. He kneeled down in front of her, pulled a harky from his back pocket and began dabbing the blood from her face. "What on earth did ya go and do, Tammy Linn?"
Most of her bloody spit drooled down her chin but a few specs dolloped on her cousin's face.

"Bobby, you're a good for nuthin' piece of" . . . she mumbled incoherently as she tried to hold her head up.

"I ain't Bobby you idiot! I'm your cousin Eddie."

The siren closed in on them and within seconds the flashing blue and red were upon them.

"Hey, man, we gotta split." Dan prepared him. "Are you cool with watching her?"

"Yeah, yeah, I got it. Thanks for . . . doin' what ya did."

Dan steered the other three in the opposite direction of the law and they made a smooth exit up the embankment and across the road.

They were walking in darkness for a minute. The commotion in the ditch was becoming faint but their nerves were tighter than the skin on a grape. All four of them were so keyed up that they were grinding their teeth.

They took a shortcut through a food shelter and came out into the light of the carnival. The rides were in motion and the game workers were barking, but people were dashing left and right. It seemed like there was disarray among the carnival patrons. Thirty feet in front of them, one of the farmers from Hicktown was kneeling on top of a much larger man from Mokane.

"What did you call me?" The Hicktown farmer dared.

"I called you a p_ _ _ y." The large and foolish man spat back.
The farmer came down with a thunderous right hand. CRACK! The large, foolish man's lower jaw fell away from the rest of his head. The farmer found his cowboy hat and strolled away.

Now the boys were bug-eyed and twitchy, shuffling along expeditiously and on high alert (no pun intended).

"Let's get on a ride." Phil chattered.

"Yeah, a long one." Steve consented.

"Not sure if I want to get on anything dangerous." Dan hinted.

"Well, let's do some games then." Brooks bantered.

"We could try, but right now I feel like an old lady in a geriatrics ward." Steve waned.

"Who has been without her meds for a week!" Dan added.

That produced a chortle among them. A much needed dose of humor to loosen them up a stitch. It didn't last long though. Directly behind them a boys voice rang out. "Over there! Let's get em!"

Their heads swiveled and in their immediate periphery was a pack of street punks closing in fast. When the boys turned around to face the pack three things were abundantly clear;
1. They were outnumbered
2. This pack was breathing hard and tattered, as if they had just been in a fight.
3. The overall atmosphere of the Mokane World's Fair at this point in time was chaotic violence.

There were skirmishes everywhere. Next to the corn dog hut were a couple of middle-aged women rolling on the ground yanking each other's hair.

"Are you guys from hicktown?" asked the leader of the pack.

The boys just nodded, knowing what was in store.

"You ain't welcome here no more." The leader followed up.

"Yeah, and we're gonna kick your ass all the way back home to mommy!" Another of the pack spewed.

"What?" Brooks defended. "All we want to do is ride some rides and have a little fun."

"You wanna have some fun . . . you gotta start with us." The leader challenged.

The fists went up and the pack started to circle.

"To hell with this!" Steve blurted. "I'm not fighting anybody."

"Come on, man," Brooks pleaded. "We can take them."

"Maybe." Steve ascertained. "Then what? They go get a few more buddies and hunt us down again?"

"I've got an idea!" Dan exclaimed and he shot out of there like a mongoose chasing a cobra. Phil, Steve and Brooks approved of his concept and said a quaint goodbye as they sprinted away from the jeers and the name calling.

Back at the near empty parking lot, they were out of breath and their mouths were dryer than the Gobi Desert. They were mindful of a large group that appeared to be chasing them in the distance but a man's got to have his priorities. Steve unlocked the trunk so they could grab a cold one before the getaway.

"What the hell? Are we the only ones left to fight?" Brooks pondered as he took a swig.

"Who cares. Get in." Steve ordered.

Gravel showered the remaining cars as Steve exited the parking lot.

The Hicktown sign, population 240, was a welcome sight for the frazzled four. It was a quiet drive to that point. Between guzzling a beverage and re-living the night's events there weren't two words spoken. Steve parked the car in front of the general store.

Dan and Brooks got out and walked up to Dan's house. Steve and Phil went home.

Phil decided he would watch some T.V., Steve opted for the comfort of his bed. Not that he was able to fall asleep within the next three hours, but at least the sun came up in the morning, negating their belief that the apocalypse was upon them.

## Wet Ride

Dan and Phil were in Dan's abused Ford Pinto on the highway outside of Hicktown. Steve and Brooks were in the Cordoba following too closely. Steve pulled beside them and Brooks fired a bottle rocket into Dan's car. A pretty amazing shot at 55 mph. Phil's cat-like reflexes saved the back seat. He pounced on it and tossed it out before it exploded. That was a two for one. Two exemplary acts in one thirty second event.

Later that night, the four Compadres were riding around the city in Dan's Pinto. When they found nothing else to do, Dan decided to put the Pinto in four-wheel drive and take a short cut to the boulevard. It was a thoroughfare that was closed due to construction. Trivial matter . . . they just moved the road blocks aside and kept on truckin'. It might have been fun if the car had been equipped with Oh-Shit handles. They bounced and shimmied until their teeth were sore and their asses were tender. They couldn't keep their beers from sloshing all over the place, so they chugged em'.

The four Compadres were only half-way to their destination and needed a break from the jackhammer effect, so Dan pulled into a car wash. "The ride is filthy and we all smell like beer, so roll your windows down and let's get cleaned up," Dan proposed.

Apparently the other three Compadres were just as drunk as Dan.

The windows went down and the feisty Pinto moved forward through the car wash.

Everyone got a whipping from the soapy flappers and a stinging from the jet spray but managed to elude the power brushes. It was the noisiest car washing ever, void of music. Between the screams and the laughter the only thing that saved them from going to jail right out of the car wash was the fact that the road was closed for construction. There wasn't a soul in sight.

When Dan finally eased out of the car wash,
Brooks was the first to realize Dan had paid for
the DELUXE WASH. He wiped the waxy film from
his lips and immediately reached for his comb to
try to keep his hair from becoming a helmet.

# The Upenleave's New House

## Dry Bluffs – Missouri 1981

Our parents' plan to buy a house, which was set in motion after the flood of 73, culminated in the erection of a pre-fabricated house in a town twenty miles North and maybe a hundred feet higher in altitude. The name of the town wasn't Dry Bluffs, but that pretty much describes the terrain.

Everyone had a hand in the process of making the weed-infested , limestone saturated, ten acre lot our new place of residence. Some of us were more instrumental than others. Donna, wasn't around much during the construction. She would soon make the move to Memphis, Tennessee for work purposes.

Fred pitched in on weekends up until the day he left for Marine Corps boot camp. Chris wasn't old enough to be useful.

Shortly after she graduated high school, Cindy found a man, got married, and started having babies. She was still in the area code though.

Denise wasn't finished traveling around the country yet. She stayed in Wisconsin for a while after high school, then moved to Colorado.

I think it would be safe to say that, other than dad, Phil and Steve spent the most time at our new property.

It was a five year venture, due to our parent's financial restrictions. We tried to undertake one project at a time, but we did almost everything ourselves. The only projects that were contracted out were; the pouring of the concrete foundation and the erection of the rock chimney, which spans the entire height of the house. Dad actually did the electrical wiring himself. Finally, in 1981, the carpet was laid and what was left of the Upenleave gang said farewell to Hicktown.

Mother was overjoyed. Father was immensely proud and full of overdue gratification. Before the new house smell had faded, he summoned his relatives to behold the crowning achievement and stay for the weekend. Mom knew it was too soon, but she couldn't talk him out of it. Apparently, Mother Nature was opposed to the hasty assemblage as well. It rained all weekend. Cardboard was put down over the carpet, but it didn't help a whole lot. By the time our relatives cleared out on Sunday, the place looked more like our farmhouse after the flood.

Needless to say, mom was having a conniption. She was sooooooo pissed off that she packed some clothes and toiletries, took her car, and moved in with Cindy and her husband.

It was during those bleak days that the four children remaining in the nest of Don and Marcia Upenleave, verified what we had suspected all those years.

In the past, we all suspected that dad was sort of, trying to be a bad cook. Something along the lines of – if you don't like your job, don't do it well.

It became obvious that our father could burn oatmeal in a microwave! Steve and Phil were damn glad to have jobs and be able to eat out during that dark interlude.

Praise the Lord, mom's hiatus only lasted a couple of weeks!

The new home (it was really new this time) was nestled on ten acres, about three miles East of a major freeway. Dry Bluffs was a small town with a population of 3,000.

After they settled in to their new community, mom and dad confronted Steve with a proposal. He needed to conform to their rules and regulations or find his own place. It seemed to mom and dad that Steve was more interested in girls and the night life than being a good role model for his young siblings.

Steve was upset that his hard labor, from digging the basement to collecting creek rocks for the chimney, was wasted!

All that work and the thanks he received was . . . being booted out before the first year of habitation was up. What the hell? It was time for him to soar anyway.

# Pony Patrol

## Dry Bluffs, Missouri - 1982

Mom and dad found a great church close by. There was a church sponsored auction on the calendar for the month. One of the items being auctioned was a pony. Dad volunteered to keep the pony on his land until auction day. Dad would rather attempt to extract honey from a four foot bee's nest in his birthday suit than be accused of doing something for somebody half-assed. In other words, dad wasn't about to allow the pony that was in his care to leave without making a substantial improvement. He had already mentioned to the priest and fellow parishioners that the pony would be broken before the auction, thereby making it more valuable.

If I haven't gotten this point across by now, I'll just flat out say it – having eight children facilitated dad into becoming the 'Arch-Duke of Delegation'.

Since fifteen year old Chris was the sole male offspring living with Mom and Dad at the time, He was the obvious choice for the dubious task at hand. Big deal that he had never ridden a horse by himself. So what if the high school basketball season was just getting underway?

Our dad was a man who enjoyed playing sports with his kids and their friends as well. He was especially fond of basketball, despite the absence of a jump shot or quickness or height for that matter.

The boys learned quickly that H-O-R-S-E was Don's game.

He might have become the first Caucasian Harlem Globetrotter had he put in the practice time because his repertoire of trick shots seemed endless. Consequently, Steve mastered the left-hand, no-lookie, reverse lay-up. Phil would challenge him with his deep base-line set shot. When Chris came of age he had all the tools to be a good basketball player. Dad encouraged him and took pride in watching him compete.

On this fine fall afternoon, dad had other priorities, so Denise, who was visiting for the weekend, volunteered to help Chris tame the pony for riding purposes. They didn't own a saddle which wasn't an immediate concern for dad. He was no stranger to bareback riding, and all he wanted to do was get the pony use to having a person onboard. Denise and Chris bridled the pony then laid a blanket over its back. There were no issues so far. Denise held the reins as Chris swung his leg over and got mounted.

If you have been around horses, you know that, especially in warm weather, they seem to have a reliable, relentless and annoying companion . . . the horse fly. This insect was undoubtedly named by a man who shoveled horse manure for a living. "Gee, I wish we could git rid o' these giant thingees what keep bothering the horses. They fly a lot so we otta call em horse flies. Yeah, that's it." If someone would have been a little more studious, he/she would have conceived a proper name. Something like . . . Unrelenting Malicious Nipper!

So Chris gently gripped the pony's mane, Denise started to walk them around when an unrelenting malicious nipper showed up to join the party.

Well, the party was right on the pony's buttocks and when the nipper nipped, the pony kicked and bucked. Chris, however, managed to keep his balance and stay aboard. He was a natural . . . until the pony reared up, jerking the reins out of Denise's hands and toppling Chris in a matter of seconds.

When Chris picked himself up his left wrist and forearm were like flesh jell-o and the shooting pains were persistent. The pony patrol had a casualty.

It wouldn't take an x-ray technician to confirm that Chris's arm was broken. The presiding IR doctor tried to reset the fracture immediately. The emphasis is on tried, here. That idiot couldn't reset an alarm clock. He looked like a spider monkey humping a football and Chris was wailing with pain. Mom was furious with the moron in the white smock but was never the type to retaliate with legal justice after-the-fact. She just gave him a tongue lashing that made him wish he was on a prep school playground instead of a professional emergency room.

The basketball season came and went without Chris. Denise felt so bad she wanted to take him out for a beer. Mom Vetoed that motion, so Denise took mom out for a beer.

Chris was more of a baseball guy anyway, and the arm was healed in time for that.

## Mobile Rockets

When Teresa was a junior in high school, she and her friend, Tina, who had been partying together in the city came home through the heart of Dry Bluffs, where they both resided.
As they cruised past the town square it was obvious to the girls that there was some activity and a couple of cute boys.

"Wanna check it out?" Teresa solicited.

"Sure, let's see what Tommy's up to."
As they pulled in to the square, a thin sparkling object struck Tina's windshield, causing her to recoil behind the wheel. Teresa whipped around to witness the explosion behind them.

"A bottle rocket!" she informed Tina.

"What the heck? Who shot that?"
The guilty party was another of their girlfriends who gave herself away by reaching into her front seat for another bottle rocket . . . and firing it at them.
"Oh hell no!" Tina exclaimed. "They just messed with the wrong beeatch!"

She directed Teresa to the glove compartment where an un-opened package of Black Cat bottle rockets illuminated the entire front seat as if it were the Holy Grail. Teresa tore the plastic from around the revenge missiles, yanked her Bic from her pocket and lit a fuse. Tina turned left into the square to afford her a clean shot.

It hit the pavement, scooting past her target by several feet, but the girl got the message. It was on!!

Another girl jumped behind the wheel and the bottle rocket sniper slid into the passenger seat. The two cars circled the square firing bottle rockets at each other with reckless abandon. Tommy and his buddy shook off the role of bystanders and hopped into his truck to get in on the action.

It was a harmless, spontaneous, very irrational exploit. I don't need to remind you that the risk of a fatal explosion when you aim fireworks at a gasoline powered vehicle is exceptionally real. Never mind that there was a **gas station within fifty feet** of the bottle rocket melee.

It did conclude in harmless fashion, with the exception of a couple of back seat / carpet burns that would have to be explained to the respective parents. Word of the amusing madness spread through the high school like a slutty girl's Friday-night frolic and would be laughed about forever afterwards.

# Right Off the Bus

## Dry Bluffs, Missouri – 1983

The usual adage for things happening instantaneously is 'right out of the gate', but a more fitting adage for our family would have been 'right off the bus!'

The school bus rolled to a stop in front of the new house and Chris was lackadaisically plodding toward the door when a boy sitting in the back alerted everybody. "Yo! I think you got a fire on your property, Upenleave!"

Chris came to life, eyes alert, panning the landscape. *"If that ten to fifteen foot blaze engulfing that thirty foot cedar tree in the back pasture is any indication,"* he thought, *"we got a problem!"*

The Roadrunner wouldn't have beat him in a race to the house. He dialed the local fire department and just as he was hanging up, Fred and Rick slid into the kitchen looking like a couple of a Kramers who had just been shot out of a cannon and landed in a coal mine.

"Did you call the fire department?" Fred stressed.

"What the hell for? I just ordered a pizza." Chris teased.

Fred was already three twitches away from a nervous breakdown and Chris sensed that the ex-Marine might be capable of inflicting severe bodily harm.

"Of course I called them. They're already on their way." Chris assured them.

Fred and Rick relaxed a bit.

Rick wearily leaned against the stove. "I need a ride to somewhere else before Don gets home." Rick was about Fred's age, twenty-two-ish. Dad befriended him at the Fulton State Hospital where dad was previously employed and Rick was ordered to reside as a troubled youth with no parents.

Rick was fifteen when he spent his first weekend at the farmhouse in Hicktown. Every once in a while he would come home with dad on Friday and go back with him on Monday.

Mentally, Rick was a little slow, but physically he was a go-getter. He thought of himself as a fine mechanic and builder of gadgets. He would lure us boys into trying to repair one of the many broken pieces of equipment that dad brought home to fix and eventually use (if he ever got the time). We would tear down a boat motor or a lawn mower engine then lose interest at some point during the re-build process. Parts and tools would be scattered all over the yard before the task was abandoned.

One of Rick's attributes was his street smarts. He is credited as our instructor for indispensable skills such as; hot wiring a vehicle and unlocking a car door with a coat hangar in less than sixty seconds.

"So what the hell happened, Guys?"
Chris pried.

"Well, Dad told us to burn a brush pile in the back. I thought it might be a little too windy, but Rick said we could handle it." Fred whined.

"I didn't say we could handle it." Rick defended.

"You did too."

"No I didn't."

"Yes you did! You said . . .

"Guys, guys, the fourteen year old interjected, does it really matter?"

Besides the establishment of blame and the bickering between Rick and Fred, there isn't a whole lot more to this story other than the culmination. The fire department ultimately put the fire out before it raged across all of our neighbor's land. There were some hard feelings between dad and the neighbors, dad and the boys, and of course, dad and mom, but everyone got over it soon after Fred and Rick got new shoes and pants. Welcome home from the Marine Corp, Fred!

## Chicken Kickin'

Months later, Chris had his first friend over to spend the night. As soon as he and his buddy, Vince, piled off of the bus, Vince had an instant fascination with all of the animals clamoring about. Chris was eager too impress his new friend and he spotted a chicken by itself in back of the house.

164

"Hey, Vince, watch this!" Chris bragged.

Chris held up his right hand, mimicking a field goal kicker, dropped it and stepped into the chicken as if it were a football. Now normally, a chicken would get flustered at being kicked with no warning or reason whatsoever and start to flap its wings.
( *don't ask me how I know* )This chicken actually played the role of a football quite admirably.
The wings stayed tucked and the chicken sailed up into a nearby tree. Vince could not believe his eyes and Chris was taken aback as well.

Had the chicken foreseen that it would nail every branch of that tree during its descent, I'm sure there would have been some flapping action right off the bus. Chris and Vince winced in unison with every WAP! and SQUAWK! After the chicken struck the final branch, miraculously, it landed on its feet made and a beeline for safety, away from the poultry al-Qeada.

"I wanna do that! Vince yelled, brimming with enthusiasm. "Can I try it next?"

## Chicken Protection

A couple of years later, when Chris had matured from a tormentor to a defender, He had a friend named Greg spending the night. Dad had been sucking up to Chris and Greg all evening. It's normal for a man to be excessively helpful and lovey-dovey to his wife when necessary.

But when a man's son and his friend are the ass-kissees, there's a storm a brewin' in the old man's mind!

Sure enough, just before sunset, father approached Chris and Greg like a military general about to bestow two heroes with the Medal of Honor.

"Boys, have you ever seen mission impossible?"

"Sure", Greg went along. "They choose to accept the mission and the tape recorder self-destructs."

"Is that all you remember about the show, Greg?" Dad questioned.

"Uhhh, pretty much."

"You're a strange bird, boy. And speaking of birds, something has been carrying off my chickens.

Have you ever shot a gun?

"Yessir. Been hunting with my dad a few times."

"You're an excellent candidate for this mission then. I would like you boys to bunk in Steve's old car   and shoot that critter if he shows up."

"You want us to sleep in that rusted out car?"

Chris mildly protested.

"I want one of you to stay awake and listen for a disturbance. You can take turns."

"Let's do it, man!" Greg chose.

So Chris and Greg slept in the rusted and busted Dodge Dart listening for a disturbance until sunrise. Greg was clearly disappointed that he didn't get to shoot anything.

Dad's chickens continued to diminish mysteriously albeit not frequently. He never ascertained what the culprit was . . . but Chris found out years later.

Chris was at a local party one night and was swapping stories with a guy named Keith who lived with his brother about two miles down the road from our new house. He confessed to Chris that every once in a while when they ran out of food and money, he would wait until dark then sneak up to Chris's house and snatch a chicken. Keith was apologetic and humble about it, but couldn't help chuckling about it in hindsight. Surprisingly, Chris laughed so hard he spilled his beer on Keith's boots.

"Damn I didn't think you would take it this well!" Keith mused.

"Well, the funny thing is, if you had snuck up there on the night me and Greg slept out in the Dodge with a twenty-two, Greg would have dropped you like a bad habit."

"Holy shit!" Keith stammered, then just walked away shaking his head and muttering to himself.

**Hot and steamy**

Now Chris had plenty of friends during his high school years but only a couple of his buddies became tight, trusting friends. Vince was one of those guys.

Growing up in a boring little town unleashed the creativity and mischievous imagination among the restless. Chris and Vince should have been co-captains of the Restless Chicken Kickers.

On this particular evening, mom and dad were playing cards at a friend's house, leaving Chris and Vince to hold down the fort. A discussion about how to occupy the evening commenced between the two boys but was cut short at the sound of someone pulling into the driveway.

Chris eased a curtain aside and turned to Vince. "It's Teresa and her boyfriend."

Silence dominated the room as the R.C.K.s pondered an inappropriate action.

"Hey," Chris piped. "let's hide in the closet and jump out and scare the hell out of them!"
        "This closet?" Vince swung the door open and scanned the three foot by two foot closet. "Gonna have to move the vacuum cleaner."
        "Grab it!"
Vince pulled it out. Chris took it from him, sprinted down the hall with it and shoved it in the corner of the spare room.

Vince slid into the closet and Chris squeezed in next to him just as the front door opened. "This is gonna be great!" Chris whispered.

Teresa and her beau entered the kitchen talking softly, tossed their belongings on the counter and started walking into the living room. Chris and Vince were shoulder-to-shoulder, Chris's hand was on the doorknob and they were primed to pounce. The beau put his arms around Teresa and began kissing her lightly on the neck. Teresa responded affectionately and the R.C.K.s had a dilemma. Vince was ready but Chris wasn't prepared to see his big sister making out just yet.

*What if the dude got mad? He probably wouldn't beat the crap out of us right here, but he would have plenty of opportunities and options to exact his revenge later, Teresa as well, for that matter.* So many scenarios were shuffling through Chris's brain, he became paralyzed.

Teresa and her boyfriend had progressed to the confines of the couch now and the make-out session started to heat up, just like the closet Chris and Vince were voluntarily trapped in.
"Just wait a minute," Chris whispered nervously. "As soon as they stand up, we're jumping out."
        "Alright, it better be soon, you jackass."

Chris and Vince waited . . . and waited . . . and waited for the love birds to take a break, but there was a high concentration of teen lust in the room that night.

169

When a person makes a bad decision, or over-analyzes the decision creating a stalemate, the clock starts ticking and the question at hand becomes – how long will he/she endure the consequences?

"To hell with this, man!" Vince blurted. Out of the closet he darted, leaving Chris the option of . . . following him. They flew up the stairs and locked themselves in Chris's room.

Teresa looked up in time to see Chris's foot. She shrugged and they resumed their semi-innocent throws of passion.

Meanwhile, Chris had to tolerate Vince's petulance toward him for such a lame idea and worse execution.

The upside was that Chris got his first life lesson to the tune of - when it comes to decision making, over-analyzation can lead to paralyzation. In this case . . . suffocation.

# The Baseball Coach

## Dry Bluffs, Missouri – 1986

Chris got a late start on his pursuit for baseball stardom. After the move from Hicktown to their new house, he lived close enough to school to participate in some extracurricular activities.

He was twelve years old when he signed up for his first little league stint. As an infielder, his lack of experience was quickly revealed. Between batters he would draw in the dirt with the toes of his cleats, which is very normal . . . for a six or seven year old.

His laid-back little league coach was tickled at Chris's infantile antics. Years of throwing a tennis ball up against the old farmhouse and catching it paid off when the coach tried him in the outfield. He seemed like a natural shagging the pop-ups. When a ball was smacked over Chris's head he reacted quickly, but as he was running toward the fence and looking back at the trajectory of the ball, his cap flew off.
    *"Can't have that. Gotta keep the uniform intact."* Chris reasoned. So he put on the brakes, went back for his cap, placed it squarely back on his head then proceeded to chase down the ball. The coach pulled him aside between innings and with an extra wide grin informed Chris that keeping his hat on wasn't all that important.

It was the summer before Chris's senior year in high school. He was involved in a summer league for baseball players.

Chris was an exceptional outfielder, but he struggled with his consistency at the plate. Admittedly, Chris was not aggressive in his tactics for extra coaching, but he spent many hours at hitting practice and played cork ball often with friends. Despite his efforts, he played three high school baseball seasons as a weak to mediocre hitter. According to Chris, dad was a very busy father. Dad was usually in the stands when Chris was on the field, but there wasn't much one-on-one interaction between games.

Chris stepped into the batters' box, looked up and spotted dad in the bleachers, then performed his pre-swing ritual. It was a summer tournament and Chris's team needed a victory to stay alive.

There were runners on second and third base in the bottom of the ninth inning and they were losing, 4 to 3. Chris watched a called strike at the knees, then a ball high and outside. The third pitch looked good, right at the belt and tailing to the outer part of the plate. Chris took a hearty cut at it and heard the contact. He dropped the bat and sped down the first base line. When he looked up, the second baseman was flipping the ball to first to end the game.

It was a damn quiet drive home . . . most of the way. Finally, dad took his hand off the wheel, placed it firmly on Chris's shoulder and broke the silence. "I think you're trying too hard, son."

"No wonder the high school coach doesn't let me hit."

"You just need to relax and don't think so much."

"I am relaxed. I'm just trying to hit it. I'm just not that good."

"Well, you're a terrific fielder. You hardly ever make an error, but I think you're swinging too hard at the plate. Why don't you just try to take a nice easy cut and turn your wrists over. Let me show you what I'm talking about when we get home?"

"I guess. I can't get any worse."

As soon as the car was parked in the driveway, dad was pulling Chris's bat out of the trunk. He squared up, bent his knees and dropped the bat from his shoulder smoothly and quickly, turning his wrists in mid-swing. He demonstrated a couple more times and verbalized his movements as well. He handed Chris the bat and watched Chris practice swinging. The wrist action was the only thing that didn't feel comfortable at first, but Chris caught-on after several practice swings and thanked dad for trying to help him.

"The most important thing is to take a nice easy swing. The ball doesn't fly based on how hard you swing, but how quick you turn your wrists and hitting the ball in the sweet part of the bat," dad informed, as they walked into the house.

About a week later Chris's team had another league game. Chris got his first chance to hit in the third inning. He stepped into the batter's box, did his pre-swing ritual then whiffed badly at a high fastball.

Chris stepped back to take a breath and dad's voice permeated the muggy air. "Remember what we talked about, son!"

Chris nodded as if to say, "Oh yeah. What do I have to lose? Nice easy swing." He took a couple of practice swings then stepped back into the batter's box. The pitcher didn't waste a second. He already knew what pitch he was going to strike Chris out with. Chris barely had time to blink before the ball came out of the pitcher's hand.

With his weight on his back leg he pivoted smoothly to his front foot as the bat moved smoothly across his chest. CRACK! There was definitely contact. Chris knew he hit it good, he saw it fly deep as he peeled out up the first base line. The last thing he saw before rounding first and heading to second was the left fielder stretching his glove out. He was still running full steam ahead when he noticed the non-chalant attitude of the shortstop approaching the base. Then he noticed the hometown crowd roar. The shortstop muttered, "it's gone bud."
Chris rounded the bases faster than most, excited and not used to rounding the bases in this fashion. His teammates were glowing as he came back to the dugout.

They were just as stunned as Chris was that he had put one out of the park, dead centerfield. As he returned to the dugout and returned his helmet to the rack, he looked over to dad, gave him a grinning, thumbs-up and shrugged his shoulders. While his teammates were happy for him, most of them considered it a fluke, a lucky swing. His next at-bat, he lined one straight back up the middle into centerfield for a single.

On his final at-bat of the day, batting eighth in the rotation, as he ambled toward the batter's box, something big happened. The opposing team's coach stepped out of the dugout and yelled to his team, "Good hitter here!" The coach instructed his outfielders to play straight up since both of Chris' hits were dead center.

It took Chris by surprise and just before he stepped into the batters' box, he took a moment to notice that coach and think about what he had said to his team. He had never experienced such an acknowledgement and his confidence went straight through the roof. He took care not to let the comment go to his head, stepped into the box and remembered what he had done the previous times.

With a nice easy swing and a quick turn of the wrists, Chris lined his third hit of the game off the centerfield wall for a double. He slid into second base ahead of the tag and one last time acknowledged dad in the stands.

His senior year of high school baseball was much different than the previous three. Confidence took the place of doubt when he stepped up to the plate. Chris was a major player in his team's run to the state championship that year. They finished third and Chris received the team's golden glove award.

The Fam in 1978

# After Words

Thank you so much for spending some of your valuable time reading my family's history. All of these events were genuine and bona fide by the person or persons in the story. In completing this manuscript I was able to preserve my family's Timeline and many precious moments, in one enjoyable project. As you can imagine, the timeline was **not** a slam dunk! It was more like . . . a double dribble, then an air ball, then a layup . . . wait . . . I got called for traveling!

Do you have an idea who the author is? It was written by a single Upenleave child. If you're curious, go to TightFam.com. Your curiosity will be satisfied on the book page.

Documenting your family's history is not a complex or arduous undertaking. Start with a casual reminiscing session with a parent or an elderly relative.
Once the stories start flowing, be prepared to take notes or record the dialogue. If you use a recorder, make sure the receiver sensitivity will pick up a moving person's voice consistently or simply handcuff the storyteller to a hard and fast object.

This may sound coldhearted but it's common sense. Get the stories from the eldest first. Your chance to interview the elderly people in your family will have vanished if you procrastinate too long. They are the roots of your tree. Their stories will launch your project and give you the momentum necessary to keep the interviews going.

I would not recommend interviewing more than two people before you start the writing process. It's not necessary to do everything chronologically, but try to get the earlier stories documented first. Once you have written a solid beginning, regardless of how many years you're covering, you can embark on more interviews.

Face-to-face is by far the most pleasurable method to get the stories, as well as being my favorite ingredient in the family history book recipe. Don't limit yourself to the in-person interview, however. Send queries for true stories via email or set up a phone interview.

Ask the person you are targeting to write a sentence or two about some humorous or adventurous events from his/her past. Give them some time to carry out this undemanding, effortless task before you threaten to poison their dog and plant land mines in their garden. Remind them on a weekly basis until they get it done, then set up the interview.

Try to get the stories written in a word processor document program as soon as possible after each interview. There will be small details lingering in the recesses of your mind that were not transcribed or verbalized sufficiently. I decided to write and save each story as a separate document in a file named . . . you guessed it . . . Family History. This allowed me to place each story into the manuscript when and where I damn well pleased.

My manuscript was done in chronological order, starting with the earliest and ending with the most recent. I did not receive or write them in that order, so having them as separate documents simplified the process of organizing the entire shebang!

Draft your back cover early on in the writing process. The reason behind this strategy is simple. Your potential reader will flip to the back cover within the first five seconds. The back cover is a snapshot of your manuscript. If you are not sure what your back cover should look like, just browse a book store or a library and see what successful authors have done or look for a style that suits you.

Your back cover should:
Possess the potential reader's attention.
Provide an enlightening snapshot of your work.
Pique the potential reader's curiosity and stimulate his/her imagination.
Set the tone for the core impression that you hope to make with your manuscript.

If, during the writing process, you lose your sense of purpose, or you are indecisive about which stories to use, peruse your back cover again. It should inspire and provide you with direction.

I know your reply to my next suggestion is going to be something like . . . Duuuuhhhhh!! But I'm going to say it anyway. Don't drag your feet when it comes to backing up your files. Save them on a CD or a memory stick right off the bus!

Here's a little scrap of wisdom that I gathered from Dan Poynter, the self-publishing guru. Don't be the writer that never finishes the manuscript.
It's easy to tell yourself "I just don't feel like it's complete. One more story and that will be it!"
Or perhaps you've lost the momentum and desire to finish the project.
One of the best ways to overcome these pitfalls is to start the printing and marketing process before you have finished writing the manuscript.

Decide on a title for your book as soon as possible. This will enable you to get an ISBN number, a barcode and a Library of Congress pre-assigned control number, all of which are mandatory for books that will be sold to the public.

Today's literary market offers many publishing options. Do some research and make a smart decision based on your financial situation and your vision for the future.

Now get to work! I am hoping to be able to relax on a gorgeous, secluded beach and bask in the hilarious moments and mischievous adventures of yours and many other's families around the world very soon!

If you would like to order more copies of
The Devious Delinquents, here are your options.

Go to Tightfam.com and order them through
PayPal for $9.95 + $2.00 for shipping.

Go to Amazon.com and search for The Devious
Delinquents or C J Upenleave. The paperback
Version is $11.95 + shipping.
The Kindle version is only $3.95

Call C J Upenleave at (913) 940 – 8747
to place an order by phone.

Devious Delinquents

www.ingramcontent.com/pod-product-compliance
Lightning Source LLC
Chambersburg PA
CBHW061433040426
42450CB00007B/1024